# PATTERNS OF THE PRESENT

# FROM THE PERSPECTIVE OF
# SRI AUROBINDO AND THE MOTHER

Georges Van Vrekhem

# Patterns of the Present

## From the Perspective of Sri Aurobindo and the Mother

*Georges Van Vrekhem*

The works of Sri Aurobindo and the Mother © Sri Aurobindo Ashram

Cover illustration: Mandelbrot set rendered by Wolfgang Beyer / Wikipedia

This book is dedicated to my Indian family

© Copyright 2012, 2002, Georges Van Vrekhem

All rights reserved. No part of this publication may be reproduced or transmitted in any form or by any means, electronic or mechanical, including photocopy, recording or any information storage and retrieval system without written permission from the publisher.

ISBN 978-1478144557

## Contents

| | |
|---|---|
| Introduction | 8 |
| 1 The Big Picture | 12 |
| 2 The Avataric Field | 36 |
| 3 East and West | 55 |
| 4 Reason on Trial | 87 |
| 5 Science, Scientism, Modern Technology | 111 |
| 6 The Supramental "Catastrophe" | 140 |
| 7 The Future of Humanity | 182 |
| *Note About the Sources* | 196 |
| *Biographical Note* | 197 |

*To hope for a true change of human life without a change of human nature is an irrational and unspiritual proposition; it is to ask for something unnatural and unreal, an impossible miracle.*

– Sri Aurobindo (*The Life Divine*, p. 1059)

*Mankind has a habit of surviving the worst catastrophes created by its own errors or by the violent turns of Nature and it must be so if there is any meaning in its existence, if its long history and continuous survival is not the accident of a fortuitously self-organising Chance, which it must be in a purely materialistic view of the nature of the world. If man is intended to survive and carry forward the evolution of which he is at present the head and, to some extent, a half-conscious leader of its march he must come out of his present chaotic international life and arrive at a beginning of organised united action; some kind of World-State, unitary and federal, or a confederacy or a coalition he must arrive at in the end; no smaller or looser expedient would adequately serve the purpose.*

– Sri Aurobindo (*The Ideal of Human Unity*, p. 585)

*All those who make an effort to overcome their ordinary nature, all those who try to realise materially the profound experience that has brought them into contact with the divine Truth, all those who, instead of turning to the Hereafter or the On-high, try to realise physically, externally, the change of consciousness they have realised within themselves – all those are apprentice-overmen.*

– the Mother (*Questions and Answers 1957-58*, p. 298)

# Introduction

Sri Aurobindo announced, in the very last months of his life, the necessity of a transitional being between man and the supramental being. This announcement was the result of his own yogic realisation in his physical being. The Mother took over this work immediately after his passing, called the transitional being *surhomme*, "overman", and realised the overmanhood in 1958. The whole effort was crowned with the establishment of the Consciousness of the overman on 1 January 1969. The development of the process, fully outlined and documented in my book *Overman: The Intermediary between the Human and the Supramental Being* (Rupa & Co), is clear, and so are the definitions and the reports of the realisations.

The importance and necessity of a transitional being, or a variety of transitional beings, is obvious considering the enormous gap between the human and the supramental being. Besides, the necessity of this intermediary step in evolution seems to agree with the normal evolutionary process in the case of the appearance in the past of every preceding species. The Mother said in 1958: "It can be affirmed with certainty that there will be an intermediate specimen between the mental and the supramental being, a kind of overman who will still have the qualities and in part the nature of man, which means that he will still belong in his most external form to the human being of animal origin, but that he will transform his consciousness sufficiently to belong, in his realisation and activity, to a new race, a race of overmen."[1]

More than a quarter of a century has passed since the Mother left her body and the avataric Yoga came to an end. The foundations of the new species, of the new Order in the world, were laid. Not only had the Supermind descended in the atmosphere

---

1. The Mother: *Questions and Answers 1957-58,* p. 277.

of the Earth, the prototype of the overman had been realised and its consciousness had become active wherever there was a receptivity, an aspiration, a turn towards the transformation of the Earth. Moreover, the Mother had realised the archetype of the supramental being.[2] So, many ask, what has become of all that in the last decades of the century and the millennium? Were there any perceptible signs of the continuation of the process? Any overmen or overwomen? Any events brought about by those new, supposedly very powerful forces? After all, one may assume that the coming of a New World is much more than a new social, scientific or religious paradigm: it means the change from a very troublesome, not to say absurd, human condition to a fully harmonious supramental, i.e. divine world. The life human would become *"the life divine"*. This would make an enormous difference necessitating a no less enormous change.

The least one can say of the 20th century is that the overall change has been, well yes, enormous. The world at the end of the century was very different from the world at its beginning, so much so that humanity has patently lost its bearings and lives in a kind of dizzying vortex, taking it ... where? Pundits made numerous comments on the advent of the new millennium, but they had little more to enunciate than commonplaces about technological inventiveness, electronic miniaturisation, artificial intelligence, interplanetary exploration and putative meetings with extraterrestrials. Change is disorienting and frightening to the human being, and humanity is afraid, now, when it takes the time to reflect on its situation. On the other hand, the effects of the technological revolution and its globalisation are so overwhelming that the planet with its inhabitants seems to be sucked, at an ever-accelerating speed, into something like a black hole.

Then, of course, there is the view of Sri Aurobindo and the Mother on the origin and destiny of the Earth and of humanity,

---

2. See Georges Van Vrekhem: *Beyond Man: The Life and Work of Sri Aurobindo and the Mother,* and *The Mother: The Story of Her Life,* both published by HarperCollins India.

and on their present development. But who will take this view as something more than sectarian or utopian? The Mother foresaw "the supramental catastrophe", as she once called in jest the great change that is now going on. In *The Life Divine* Sri Aurobindo had already written: "When the turning point has been reached, the decisive line crossed, the new life in its beginnings would have to pass through a period of ordeal and arduous development."[3] Things cannot change, even for the better, without changing. Evolution has progressed through a clash of forces. Yet "the supramental has a greater – in its fullness a complete mastery of things and power of harmonisation which can overcome resistance by other means than dramatic struggle and violence ... As far as I can see", wrote Sri Aurobindo, "once the supramental is established in Matter, the transformation will be possible under much less troublesome conditions than now are there. These bad conditions are due to the fact that the Ignorance is in possession and the hostile Powers an established authority, as it were, who do not care to give up their hold ..."[4]

"The world knows three kinds of revolution. The material has strong results, the moral and intellectual are infinitely large in their scope and richer in their fruits, but the spiritual are the great sowings."[5] We are at present fully involved in the greatest, not to say the ultimate spiritual revolution. "The changes we see in the world today [i.e. around 1920] are intellectual, moral, physical in their ideal and intention. The spiritual revolution waits for its hour and throws up meanwhile its waves here and there. Until it comes the sense of the others cannot be understood and till then all interpretation of present happening and forecast of man's future are vain things. For its nature, power, event are that which will determine the next cycle of our humanity."[6] The definitive spiritual revolution is underway, now; it is what is happening all around us, everywhere. Since

---

3. Sri Aurobindo: *The Life Divine*, p. 1061.
4. Sri Aurobindo: *Letters on Yoga,* pp. 34-35.
5. Sri Aurobindo: *Essays in Philosophy and Yoga*, p. 210.
6. Id., p. 211.

*Introduction*

1956 it cannot but be underway, for the Supermind, manifested in the earth-consciousness in that year, cannot but be active. Its action, though, has to be prudently dosed not to cause too much damage and therefore takes some time to be apparent.

In 1972 the Mother said that there was "a golden Force" exerting pressure on the Earth, so heavily that catastrophes seemed inevitable. But as this was the supramental Force, harmonious and all-powerful, time and again a solution cropped up in circumstances that seemed miraculous, she added.[7] This is what, at present, is causing our world to spin so wildly and what, at the same time, is ensuring that apparent chaos may lead towards the right outcome. This is a change so great that the way to bring it about must of necessity be drastic and bewildering to the human mind.

What follows are notes, reflections, quotations, comments and comparisons, all in connection with the continuation of the transformative process caused by the fundamental realisations of Sri Aurobindo and the Mother, and with the spiritual Forces active at present. To make these notes and reflections more readable, they have been organised around some of the main topics, chosen as themes of the chapters.

---

7. *Mother's Agenda*, 6 May 1972.

# 1
# The Big Picture

*Always he is the traveller of the cycles and his road is forward.*[1]

– SRI AUROBINDO

## Spiralling Upwards

If the global change now in progress has the importance Sri Aurobindo and the Mother ascribed to it, it must be seen in a much larger perspective than the academic historians are willing to accept. Only when perceived in the context of humanity and its evolution, of our planet Earth and its evolution, and therefore of the universe, can one begin to grasp what the present transition from "the lower hemisphere" of Ignorance, Falsehood and Darkness to "the higher hemisphere" of Knowledge, Truth and Light actually means.

It is often thought that Sri Aurobindo and the Mother's view of evolution was straightforwardly linear. But simple linearity, like flawless symmetry, is a typical child of the human mind, of the intellectual interpretation and ordering of things. More than once one meets in Sri Aurobindo phrases like "much too symmetrical to be true" and warnings against erring by rigidity and substituting "a mental straight line for the coils and zigzags of Nature"[2]. ("Nature" in Sri Aurobindo and the Mother's writings is always a concrete Being, in fact an emanation or

---
1. Sri Aurobindo: *The Human Cycle,* p. 67.
2. Id., p. 2.

## 1. The Big Picture

personality of the Universal Mother charged with the manifestation of the universe and everything in it.) The unity of the Truth that is All can to our mind only be represented as global. This too is a metaphor and a symbol, of course, but the one that is best suited to represent the unthinkable, the unfathomable to mental beings like us.

"The idea of human progress itself is very probably an illusion", writes Sri Aurobindo taking the broad view, "for there is no sign that man, once emerged from the animal stage, has radically progressed during his race-history;[3] at most he has advanced in knowledge of the physical world, in Science in the handling of his surroundings, in his purely external and utilitarian use of the secret laws of Nature. But otherwise he is what he always was in the early beginnings of civilisation; he continues to manifest the same capacities, the same qualities and defects, the same efforts, blunders, achievements, frustrations. *If progress there has been, it is in a circle, at most perhaps a widening circle.* Man today is not wiser than the ancient seers and sages and thinkers, not more spiritual than the great seekers of old, the first mighty mystics, not superior in arts and crafts to the ancient artists and craftsmen." Didn't a recent expert opinion tell us that art has not improved on the wall paintings at Lascaux? And Sri Aurobindo continues: *"The old races that have disappeared* showed as potent an intrinsic originality, invention, capacity of dealing with life and, if modern man in this respect has gone a little farther, not by any essential progress but in degree, scope, abundance, it is because he has inherited the achievements of his forerunners.

---

[3]. "If a hominid with a human foot existed more than three million years ago, it would certainly add useful support to the argument of this book – that civilisation is thousands of years older than historians believe. At first sight that statement may sound absurd – what difference can a few thousand years make, when we are speaking in millions? But what is really at issue here is the development of the human mind. In *Timescale*, Nigel Calder quotes the anthropologist T. Wynn to the effect that tests devised by the psychologist Jean Piaget, carried out on Stone Age tools from Isimila, Tanzania – whose uranium dating shows them to be 330,000 years old – *indicate that the makers were as intelligent as modern humans.*" Colin Wilson: *From Atlantis to the Sphinx*, p. 203 (emphases in the text).

Nothing warrants the idea that he will ever hew his way out of the half-knowledge, half-ignorance which is the stamp of his kind, or, even if he develops a higher knowledge, that he can break out of the boundary of the mental circle"[4].

Nonetheless, in *The Life Divine* he also writes: "It may be conceded that what man has up till now principally done is to act within the circle of his nature, on a spiral of nature-movement, sometimes descending, sometimes ascending, – there has been no straight line of progress, no indisputable, fundamental or radical exceeding of his past nature: what he has done is to sharpen, subtilise, make a more and more complex and plastic use of his capacities. It cannot truly be said that there has been no such thing as human progress since man's appearance or even in his recent ascertainable history; for however great the ancients, however supreme some of their achievements and creations, however impressive their powers of spirituality, of intellect or of character, there has been in later developments an increasing subtlety, complexity, manifold development of knowledge and possibility in man's achievements. In his politics, society, life, science, metaphysics, knowledge of all kinds, art, literature; even in his spiritual endeavour, less surprisingly lofty and less massive in power of spirituality than that of the ancients, there has been this increasing subtlety, plasticity, sounding of depths, extension of seeking.

"*There have been falls from a high type of culture, a sharp temporary descent into a certain obscurantism, cessations of the spiritual urge, plunges into a barbaric natural materialism;* but these are temporary phenomena, at worst a downward curve of the spiral of progress. This progress has not indeed carried the race beyond itself, into a self-exceeding, a transformation of the mental being. But that was not to be expected; for the action of evolutionary Nature in a type of being and consciousness is first *to develop the type to its utmost capacity* by just such a subtilisation and increasing complexity till it is ready for her bursting of the shell, the ripened

---

4. Sri Aurobindo: *The Life Divine*, p. 832.

decisive emergence, reversal, turning over of consciousness on itself that constitutes a new stage in the evolution ...

"If the appearance in animal being of a type similar in some respects to the ape-kind but already from the beginning endowed with the elements of humanity was the method of the human evolution, the appearance in the human being of a spiritual type resembling mental-animal humanity but already with the stamp of the spiritual aspiration on it would be the obvious method of Nature for the evolutionary production of the spiritual and supramental being."[5] This, now, is the privileged moment of the bursting of the shell, of the ripened decisive emergence, of the great reversal in consciousness; it is the moment of the appearance of the overman, enabling the embodiment of the superman.

"We believe in the constant progression of humanity and we hold that that progression is the working out of a Thought in Life which sometimes manifests itself on the surface and sometimes sinks below and works behind the mask of external forces and interests. When there is this lapse below the surface, humanity has its periods of apparent retrogression or tardy evolution, its long hours of darkness or twilight during which the secret Thought behind works out one of its phases by the pressure mainly of economic, political and personal interests ignorant of any deeper aim within. When the Thought returns to the surface, humanity has its periods of light and rapid efflorescence, its dawns and splendid springtides, and according to the depth, vitality, truth and self-effective energy of the form of Thought that emerges is the importance of the stride forward that it makes during these Hours of the Gods in our terrestrial manifestation."[6]

Sri Aurobindo wrote about the cyclic movement of the evolution of humanity: "In the history of man everything seems now to point to alternations of a serious character, ages of

---

5. Id., pp. 841-42, emphases added.
6. Sri Aurobindo: *Essays in Philosophy and Yoga*, p. 140. See also the beautiful, biblically prophetic sounding text by Sri Aurobindo: *The Hour of God*, in *Essays Divine and Human*.

progression, ages of recoil, the whole constituting an evolution that is cyclic rather than in one straight line. A theory of cycles of human civilisation has been advanced[;] we may yet arrive at the theory of cycles of human evolution, the *Kalpa* and *Manwantaras* of the Hindu theory. If its affirmation of cycles of world-existence is farther off from affirmation, it is because they must be so vast in their periods as to escape not only all means of observation, but all our means of deduction or definite inference."[7] According to the Hindu scriptures, the four Ages or yugas are the *Krita* or Golden Age, the *Treta* or Silver Age, the *Dwapara* or Bronze Age and the *Kali* or Iron Age. Together they cover the enormous span of 4,310,000 (human) years. (Hindu scripture also speaks about a "year of Brahman" which equals 360 human years.)

"Every world creation begins in the perfection of the Krita Age, progressively deteriorates throughout the *Treta* and *Dwapara* until the final destruction comes at the end of every *Kali* – only to give way once more to a recreation in a new *Krita*, and so on."[8] Talking about the cycles, the Mother once used the occult symbol of a Snake biting its own tail. In the course of the cycles there is "a progressive descent from the most subtle to the most material."[9] The end of the *Kali* Yuga represents the most material point in the whole development, specifically on the Earth, which, as we will see, occupies a very special place in the universe. As a new Golden Age will follow the Iron Age, it is precisely at this end – the point where the Snake bites its tail – that the Work of change to enter the Golden Age can be done in its most concentrated and most effective form.

The cycles of the human evolution are not exact and eternal repetitions of a given sequence of events, as is for instance Nietzsche's "eternal return", but "cycles of a growing but still imperfect harmony and synthesis". Nature brings man back "violently to her original principles, sometimes even to something

---

7. Sri Aurobindo: *Essays in Philosophy and Yoga,* pp. 173-74.
8. Cornelia Dimmitt and J.A.B. van Buitenen: *Classical Hindu Mythology,* p. 21.
9. The Mother: *Questions and Answers 1953,* p. 275.

## 1. The Big Picture

like her earlier conditions so that he may start afresh on a larger curve of progress and self-fulfilment."[10] The spiralling movement is double: widening, to include ever larger portions of the divine manifestation, and upward, towards the divine perfection.

"There have been beautiful civilisations like the one which left something like an occult memory of a continent that might have linked India with Africa and of which no trace remains – unless certain human races be the remnants of that civilisation", said the Mother. "There are civilisations like that which disappear suddenly and which are followed by a long period full of darkness, inconscience, ignorance, with very primitive races apparently so close to the animals that one asks oneself whether there is really any difference. And so there is there a big dark hole and [humanity] has to pass through upheavals of all kinds. But then, all of a sudden, there emerges something at the top, something higher than before, with greater qualities, a greater realisation – as though all the time spent in the night and of work in the night had prepared Matter so that it might express something higher. Then again another darkness, oblivion: the earth again becomes barbarous, obscure, ignorant, wretched. And some thousands of years later suddenly a new civilisation emerges.[11] – Until now one has always fallen back.[12]" It was the Mother and Sri Aurobindo's constant endeavour to found their supramental creation "to front the years", in a way that there would not be any falling back this time, or as Sri Aurobindo put it "not to repeat the old fiasco".

More than once the Mother recalled what her former teacher, Max Théon, had told her in the foothills of the Atlas Mountains: "The traditions say that a universe is created, then withdrawn in *pralaya*[13]; then a new one appears, and so on. And according to them we should be the seventh universe, and being the seventh

---
10. Sri Aurobindo: *The Human Cycle*, p. 83.
11. The Mother: *Questions and Answers 1953*, pp. 249-50.
12. The Mother: *Notes on the Way,* p. 311.
13. In Hinduism, *pralaya* is an act of the Supreme by which He withdraws his whole manifestation (creation) into Himself.

universe we are the one that will not return into *pralaya* but progress continuously without ever drawing back. It is because of this, moreover, that there is in the human being this need of permanence and of an uninterrupted progress: it is because the time has come."[14] But she said also, when battling in the swamps of the subconscious: "In the subconscious there is the memory of bygone *pralayas,* so it is this memory that always gives the feeling that everything will be dissolved, that everything will collapse."[15]

## Times Before History

"Not one hundred-thousandth part of what has been has still a name preserved by human Time,"[16] wrote Sri Aurobindo, who was never given to exaggeration, in a letter to a disciple. In the *Arya* he had already written: "Emerging from the periods of eclipse and the nights of ignorance which overtake humanity, we assume always that we are instituting new knowledge. In reality, we are continually rediscovering the knowledge and repeating the achievement of the ages that have gone before us, – receiving again out of the 'Inconscient' the light that it had drawn back into its secrecies and now releases once more for a new day and another march of the great journey."[17] His very reasonable argument in this is that the ten thousand years of our "official" history cannot suffice to develop the human mind from primitivism to the capacity of civilisation. "The time-limit allowed for the growth of civilisation is still impossibly short and in consequence an air of unreality hangs over the application of the evolutionary idea to our human development."[18] The Mother, on her side, confirmed that "the historic period is

---

14. The Mother: *Questions and Answers 1950-51,* p. 23.
15. The Mother: *Notes on the Way,* p. 311.
16. Sri Aurobindo: *Letters on Yoga,* p. 456.
17. *Arya,* vol. 2, p. 120.
18. *Sri Aurobindo Archives and Research,* vol. 3 no. 1, p. 94.

too short". We have already seen her reference to a continent that might have linked India with Africa and of which no trace remains. "Very long ago there have been great and beautiful civilisations perhaps as advanced materially as ours. Looked at from a certain standpoint, the most modern culture seems no more than a repetition of ancient cultures ..."[19] she said in 1929. And in 1951, under the threat of a third world war, she said: "There have been many civilisations on the Earth. There are scientists who try to rediscover what has been, but nobody can say for certain what was there. The major part of those civilisations is completely lost. I am speaking of civilisations preceding the one that is for us historical. Well, if thousands of years would again be needed to start another one ... But we have been told that the Work to be done, that the promised Realisation is going to take place now. It is going to take place now because the framework of the present civilisation seems favourable as a platform or a base for building upon. But if this civilisation is destroyed, upon what are we going to build? First the ground must be prepared to be able to build ..."[20] Science is pushing back the time of the origin of the human species nearly every five years, and the fact that there have been civilisations which disappeared from the surface of the Earth seems irrefutable to anybody with an open mind. From where did the suddenly flourishing civilisation of Egypt get its amazing theoretical and practical knowledge – a knowledge that after a resplendent beginning gradually deteriorated? Another case in point: "The evidence presented by the ancient maps appears to suggest the existence in remote times, before the rise of any known cultures, of a true civilisation of an advanced kind, which either was localised in one area but had worldwide commerce, or was, in a real sense, a *worldwide* culture. This culture, at least in some respects, was more advanced than the civilisation of Greece and Rome. In geodesy, nautical science, and mapmaking it was more advanced than any known culture before the 18th century of

---

19. The Mother: *Questions and Answers 1929*, p. 26.
20. The Mother: *Questions and Answers 1950-51*, p. 330.

the Christian Era. It was only in the 18th century that we developed practical means of finding longitude. It was in the 18th century that we first accurately measured the circumference of the earth. Not until the 19th century did we begin to send out ships for exploration into the Arctic or Antarctic Seas and only then did we begin the exploration of the bottom of the Atlantic. The maps indicate that some ancient people did all these things ... More than a quarter of a century after its publication, the evidence of Hapgood's book [*Maps of the Ancient Sea Kings*, 1966] remains as solid and unshaken as ever."[21] This agrees with what Sri Aurobindo had to say in an unfinished essay written before 1914: "The time-limit allowed for the growth of civilisation is still impossibly short and in consequence an air of unreality hangs over the application of the evolutionary idea to our human development. Nor is this essential objection cured by any evidence of the modernity of human civilisation. Its great antiquity is denied merely on the absence [of] affirmative data; there are no positive indications to support the denial; but where data are scanty, such a negative basis is in the last degree unsound and precarious. We can no longer argue that no ancient civilisations can have existed of which the traces have entirely perished and that prehistoric means, necessarily, savage and undeveloped. History on the contrary abounds with instances of great societies which were within an ace of disappearing without leaving any visible memorial behind them, and recent excavations have shown that such disappearances in ancient times have been even not uncommon. We cannot have exhausted all that the earth contains.[22] There should be the remains of other civilisations yet undiscovered and there may well have been yet others which because of the manner of

---

21. Colin Wilson: *From Atlantis to the Sphinx*, pp. 98-99.
22. The meaning of this sentence seems to be exactly what the present chapter is about: that the potential of humanity is intrinsically much larger than perceived in the recent, known civilisations, and that previous cycles were a necessity to realise this potential and make the transition possible from the lower hemisphere of Darkness to the higher hemisphere of Light.

their disappearance or for other causes have left no traces at all whether upon the surface of the earth or under it."[23]

"Our observation is bad because, prepossessed by the fixed idea of a brief and recent emergence from immemorial barbarism, imagining Plato to have blossomed in a few centuries out of a stock only a little more advanced than the South Sea islander, we refuse to seek in the records that still remain of a lost superior knowledge their natural and coherent significance", writes Sri Aurobindo. "We twist them rather into the image of our own thoughts or confine them within the still narrow limits of what we ourselves know and understand. The logical fallacy we land in as the goal of our bad observation is the erroneous conception that because we are more advanced than certain ancient peoples in our own especial lines of success, as the physical science, therefore necessarily we are also more advanced in other lines where we are still infants and have only recently begun to observe and experiment, as the science of psychology and the knowledge of our subjective existence and of mental forces. Hence we have developed the exact contrary of the old superstition that the movement of man is always backward to retrogression."[24]

There seem to be three principles of discovery at least as reliable as Murphy's Law: every line of discovery broadens from the limited to the boundless, from the simple to the complex, from the imaginable to the mind-boggling. This has been valid for all branches of discovery pursued by the positive sciences in their exploration of the cosmos, the planet, the living beings, the body, the cell, the atomic and subatomic world, etc. It will be equally valid for the inner worlds, their beings, man, the soul of man, the occult and spiritual capacities of man, and his possibilities of transformation. Science has remained limited by its dominant principle of positivist materialism. The "future science", as foreseen by Sri Aurobindo and the Mother, will

---

23. Sri Aurobindo: *Essays Divine and Human*, p. 382.
24. *Sri Aurobindo Archives and Research*, vol. 3 no. 1, p.93.

break through the barrier of what is perceptible by the senses, and will proceed "from within outwards".

A certain awareness of the vastness of human time before our recorded period of history is a necessity to realise the importance of "the giant point" at which the evolutionary development has now arrived. For if it is true that we are in a period of transition from the lower to the higher hemisphere of existence, then *homo sapiens* must have exerted and exhausted all his possibilities, which may have been much more varied and richer than we, judging by our present capacities, suppose. Just as every Avatar takes up the whole past of humanity in order to bring it a step further, now humanity itself must take up its whole past to go beyond itself, at least in some of its representatives: the present overmen and overwomen.

The working out of all its capacities may be the reason that humanity had to regress time and again in order to attain "to something higher than before", as the Mother said. Sri Aurobindo is quite positive about this frequent regression. Writing for instance about the still existing primitive stages of the human development, he made the proviso: "... if it is indeed such [i.e. primitive] and not, in what we still see of it, a fall or vestige, a relapse from a higher knowledge belonging to a previous cycle of civilisation or the debased remnants of a dead or obsolete culture ..."[25] This would explain many of the mysteries now covered by forests, deserts and oceans. "The savage is perhaps not so much the first forefather of civilised man as the degenerate descendant of a previous civilisation ... Barbarism is an intermediate sleep, not an original darkness ..."[26]

The following text on this topic by Sri Aurobindo, part of a commentary on the *Isha Upanishad,* deserves to be quoted extensively. "The Puranic account supposes us to have left behind the last Satya period, the age of harmony, and to be now in a period of enormous breakdown, disintegration and increasing confusion in which man is labouring forward towards a new

---

25. Sri Aurobindo: *The Life Divine*, p. 869.
26. Sri Aurobindo: *The Synthesis of Yoga*, pp. 9 and 10.

## 1. The Big Picture

harmony which will appear when the spirit of God descends again upon mankind in the form of the *Avatara* called *Kalki*, destroys all that is lawless, dark and confused and establishes the reign of the saints, the Sadhus, those, that is to say, – if we take the literal meaning of the word Sadhu, – who are strivers after perfection. Translated, again, into modern language more rationalistic but, again, let me say, not necessarily more accurate, this would mean that the civilisation by which we live is not the result of a recent hotfooted gallop forward from the condition of the Caribbee and Hottentot, but the detritus and uncertain reformation of a great era of knowledge, balance and adjustment which lives for us only in tradition, but in a universal tradition, the Golden Age, the *Saturnia regna*, of the West, our *Satyayuga* or age of the recovered Veda.

"What then are these savage races, these epochs of barbarism, these Animistic, Totemistic, Naturalistic and superstitious beliefs, these mythologies, these propitiatory sacrifices, these crude conditions of society? Partly, the Hindu theory would say, the ignorant fragmentary survival of defaced and disintegrated beliefs and customs, originally deeper, simpler, truer than the modern, – even as a broken statue by Phidias or Praxiteles or a fragment of an Athenian dramatist is at once simpler and nobler or more beautiful and perfect than the best work of the moderns, – partly, a reeling back into the beast, an enormous movement of communal atavism brought about by worldwide destructive forces in whose workings both Nature and man have assisted.

"Animism is the obscure memory of an ancient discipline which put us into spiritual communion with intelligent beings and forces living behind the veil of gross matter sensible to our limited material organs. Nature worship is another side of the same ancient truth. Fetishism remembers barbarously the great Vedic dogma that God is everywhere and God is all and that the inert stone and rock, things mindless and helpless and crude, are also He; in them, too, there is the intelligent Force that has built the Himalayas, filled with its flaming glories the sun and arranged the courses of the planets. The mythologies are ancient traditions, allegories and symbols. The savage and the cannibal are merely the human beast, man hurled down from this ascent and returning from the *sattwic* or intelligent state into the tamasic, crumbling into the animal and almost into the clod by that disintegration through inertia which to the Hindu idea is the ordinary road to disappearance into the vague and rough material of Nature out of which we were made. The ascent of man, according to this theory, is not a facile and an assured march; on the contrary, it is a steep, a strenuous effort, the ascent difficult, though the periods of attainment and rest yield to us ages of golden joy, the descent frightfully easy."[27]

## *"A Habitable Planet in an Inhabitable System"*[28]

> *This earth alone is not our teacher and nurse;*
> *The powers of all the worlds have entrance here.*[29]

"[Sri Aurobindo] does not take the whole universe into account", said the Mother when commenting upon a passage of *The Life Divine*. "He has taken terrestrial life, that is, our life here, on the Earth, as a symbolic and concentrated representation of the *raison d'être* of the entire universe. In fact, according to very old traditions, the Earth, from the deeper spiritual point of view, has been created as a symbolic concentration of universal life so that the work of transformation may be done more easily, in a limited, concentrated "space", so to say, where all the elements of the problem are gathered together so that, in this concentration, the action may be more total and effective."[30]

On another occasion she said: "The universe is an objectivation of the Supreme, as if he had objectivised himself outwardly in order to see himself, to experience himself, to know himself,

---

27. *Sri Aurobindo Archives and Research,* vol. 7 no. 1, pp. 116-17.
28. Sri Aurobindo: *The Superman,* in *The Supramental Manifestation Upon Earth,* SABCL, p. 226.
29. Sri Aurobindo: *Savitri,* p. 153.
30. The Mother: *Questions and Answers 1957-58,* p. 209.

and so that there might be an existence and a consciousness capable of recognising him as their origin and of uniting consciously with him to manifest him in the becoming. There is no other reason for the universe. The Earth is a kind of symbolic crystallisation of universal life, a reduction, a concentration, so that the work of evolution may be easier to do and follow. And if we consider the history of the Earth, we can understand why the universe has been created. It is the Supreme growing aware of himself in an eternal Becoming; and the goal is the union of the created with the Creator, a union that is conscious, voluntary and free, in the Manifestation."[31]

Sri Aurobindo and the Mother have restored the Earth to its former central place in the cosmos, not physically but symbolically. It is the *bhumi*, the place of material evolution. After Copernicus and at a time when the search for extraterrestrial life is one of the fads of official science, this may come as something like a shock. Or rather it might have come as a shock in 1957, at the time the above quotations were spoken. In recent years the experts seemed to be changing their opinions. John Horgan, for instance, former senior writer at *Scientific American* and the author of the influential *The End of Science* and *The Undiscovered Mind*: "Physicists think that the existence of a highly technological civilisation here on earth makes the existence of similar civilisations elsewhere highly probable. The real experts on life – biologists – find this view ludicrous, because they know how much plain luck is involved in evolution. Harvard palaeontologist Stephen Jay Gould has said that if the great experiment of life were re-run a million times over, chances are it would never again give rise to mammals, let alone mammals intelligent enough to invent television."[32]

(Gould's opinion, however, is limited, for it takes gross material evolution as the only possibility. According to Sri Aurobindo and the Mother there is life everywhere in the universe, but in different shapes and densities of substance, generated by and

---

31. Id., p. 321.
32. *Time Special Issue*, January 1998, p. 101.

adapted to the heavenly body on which it originated. When the Mother touched upon this subject in a private conversation, she said that "even our way of thinking depends on our form", and that nothing allows us to suppose that life elsewhere should be similar to the life form we know and are. "There is only one thing, one vibration that seems to be really universal: the vibration of Love."[33])

Another quotation in this context is from Charles Panati, formerly head physicist at RCA and a *Newsweek* science editor. "Preposterous as it sounds, and despite the statistical evidence against it, the pre-Copernican idea that we are the centre of the universe has regained popularity. Proposed by cosmologist George Ellis of the University of Cape Town, the theory is unacceptably anthropocentric, yet, surprisingly, it does not violate current astronomical observations ... Curiously enough, just when (or because?) so many scientists are searching for evidence of extraterrestrial intelligence (ETI), a number of astronomers and biologists are becoming increasingly vocal about the possibility of the existence of ETI being infinitesimally small. Some have gone so far as to recall the centuries-old notion, now referred to as the 'anthropic principle' that we are alone in the universe. 'The chances are overwhelming,' says physicist John Wheeler, 'that the earth is the sole outpost of life in the universe.'"[34] It should be noted again that Sri Aurobindo and the Mother never say that the Earth is the topographical centre of the universe, but its "symbolic" centre, and that according to them extraterrestrial life abounds, though not in our familiar gross material form.

"The formation of the Earth as we know it – this infinitesimal point in the immense universe – was made precisely in order to concentrate the transformational effort upon one point", said the Mother. "It is as if it were a symbolic point created in the universe to be able to radiate the work, done upon this one point, into the entire universe ... From the astronomical point

---

33. *Mother's Agenda*, 18 June 1966.
34. Charles Panati: *Breakthroughs*, pp. 242-43.

## 1. The Big Picture

of view the Earth is nothing, it is a very small accident. From the spiritual point of view [however] it is a voluntary symbolic formation. And as I already said, it is only upon the Earth that the Presence is found, the direct contact with the supreme Origin, the presence of the divine Consciousness hidden in all things. The other worlds were organised more or less 'hierarchically', if one may put it like that, but the Earth has a special formation due to the direct intervention, without any intermediary, of the supreme Consciousness in the Inconscient ... I have taken care to tell you that that emanation [i.e. the formation of the Earth] was a symbolic creation, and that all action on this special point radiates out into the whole universe. Don't forget this, and don't start saying that the cause of the formation of the Earth was some part projected from the sun, or that a scattering nebula gave birth to the sun and all its satellites, or whatever."[35]

Later the Mother repeated this and added: "For the convenience and necessity of the Work, the whole universe was concentrated and condensed symbolically in a grain of sand which is called the Earth. On it there is the symbol of everything. Everything that is to be changed, everything that is to be transformed, everything that is to be converted, is here. This means that if one concentrates on this work and does it here, all the rest will follow automatically. Otherwise there would be no end to it – and no hope."[36] That this was not merely a supposition or a theoretical point – Sri Aurobindo and the Mother were always practical – is proven by the fact that she reiterated this point several times in the course of the years. "By transforming the Earth one can, through 'contagion' or analogy, transform the universe, for the Earth is the symbol of the universe."[37] Thus was the Earth rehabilitated.

As the Mother said: "It is only upon the Earth that the Presence is found ... the presence of the divine Consciousness hidden in all things." This presence is the psychic presence, and her words mean that only the beings on the Earth have a soul.

---
35. The Mother: *Questions and Answers 1950-51,* p. 242.
36. The Mother: *Questions and Answers 1953,* p. 276.
37. The Mother: *Questions and Answers 1955,* p. 91.

To put it more clearly – for the soul is one of the least understood issues in religion and philosophy, especially in the West – the divine Consciousness is present, "hidden", in everything upon the Earth; in beings belonging to the vital world, even the amoeba and the snail, this Presence may be called "the divine spark"; in human beings there is an evolving "psychic being" with the divine spark as its core and growing around it. It is the psychic being that makes the human specifically human and that takes on the various *adharas* on its way to supermanhood or divinity. Supermanhood becomes possible when the psychic being is fully developed, i.e. when it has gone through the whole cycle of incarnations and consciously becomes what it eternally was and is in its Origin.

"All knowledge in all traditions, in any part of the Earth, says that the psychic formation is a terrestrial formation, and that the growth of the psychic being is something that takes place upon Earth. But once they [i.e. the psychic beings] are fully formed and free in their movement, they can go anywhere in the universe, they are not limited in their movement. But their formation and growth belong to the terrestrial life, for reasons of concentration."[38] – "One thing is certain: that this marvellous fact of the divine Presence in Matter, which is at the origin of the formation of the psychic being, belongs as such to life on the Earth."[39] – "In the whole creation the Earth has a place of distinction, because unlike any other planet it is evolutionary with a psychic being at its centre."[40]

The Mother has forcefully asserted at the time a nuclear war was a real possibility that "the Earth will not disappear", meaning that it will go on existing to make that full development of its evolution possible. After its transformation, its divinisation, the possibility of its disappearance does not even exist any more. "The Earth will not be destroyed", she said.[41]

---

38. The Mother: *Questions and Answers 1950-51*, p. 243.
39. The Mother: *Questions and Answers 1956*, p. 35.
40. *Words of the Mother*, CMW 13, p. 376.
41. *Mother's Agenda*, 23.7.1960 and 11.12.1971.

Earth is the chosen place of mightiest souls;
Earth is the heroic spirit's battlefield,
The forge where the Archmason shapes his works.
Thy servitudes on earth are greater, King,
Than all the glorious liberties of heaven.[42]

## The Human Cycle

Are the astronomical figures that determine the Yugas in the Hindu mythology to be taken literally? "Too much weight need not be put on the exact figures about the Yugas in the Purana. Here again the Kala and the Yugas indicate successive periods in the cyclic wheel of evolution, – the perfect state, decline and disintegration of successive ages of humanity followed by a new birth – the mathematical calculations are not the important element. The argument of the end of the *Kali Yuga* already come or coming and a new *Satya Yuga* coming is a very familiar one and there have been many who have upheld it."[43] The last sentence may be seen as Sri Aurobindo's way of confirming the argument. Practically speaking, the important point is the actual, momentous transition from the *Kala* to the *Satya* Yuga. It is the fundamental sense of our lives at present on this planet – the point where the Snake of Time bites its own tail.

In *The Human Cycle*, a sociological work of the first order, Sri Aurobindo proposes another cycle of human evolution from the Satya to the *Kala Yuga* and beyond. The idea came to him when reading Karl Lamprecht (1856-1915), "one of the first scholars to develop a systematic theory of psychological factors in history". Lamprecht "supposed that human society progresses through certain distinct psychological stages which he terms respectively symbolic, typal and conventional, individualist and subjective ... Obviously, such classifications are likely to err by rigidity and

---
42. Sri Aurobindo: *Savitri*, p. 686.
43. Sri Aurobindo: *Letters on Yoga*, p. 403.

to substitute a mental straight line for the coils and zigzags of Nature."[44] Sri Aurobindo widened the scope of the classification and adapted it to his own view.

"Wherever we can seize human society in what to us seems its primitive beginnings or early stages ... we do find a strongly *symbolic* mentality that governs or at least pervades its thought, customs and institutions. Symbolic, but of what? We find that this social stage is always religious and actively imaginative in its religion; for symbolism and a widespread imaginative or intuitive religious feeling have a natural kinship and especially in earlier or primitive formations they have gone always together ... The symbol then is of something which man feels to be present behind himself and his life and his activities – the Divine, the Gods, the vast and deep unnameable, a hidden, living and mysterious nature of things. All his religious and social institutions, all the moments and phases of his life are to him symbols in which he seeks to express what he knows or guesses of the mystic influences that are behind his life and shape and govern or at the least intervene in its movements."[45] The word "religious" in this context clearly does not have the common meaning connected with a dogmatic, institutional religion, but rather means what now we would call "spiritual".

As an example of the symbolic mentality Sri Aurobindo gives "the far-off Vedic age which we no longer understand", precisely because the symbolic mentality is no longer ours and much has come in between. (There is no known example in the West, except perhaps to some extent the ancient Gallic, druidic society or societies.) "The theory that there was nothing in the sacrifice except a propitiation of Nature-gods for the gaining of worldly prosperity and of Paradise, is a misunderstanding by a later humanity which had already become profoundly affected by an intellectual and practical bent of mind, practical even in its religion and even in its own mysticism and symbolism, and therefore could no longer enter into the ancient spirit ... From

---

44. Sri Aurobindo: *The Human Cycle*, p. 6.
45. Id., pp. 7 and 8 (emphasis added).

## 1. The Big Picture

this symbolic attitude came the tendency to make everything in society a sacrament, religious and sacrosanct, but as yet with a large and vigorous freedom in all its forms ... The spiritual idea governs all; the symbolic religious forms which support it are fixed in principle; the social forms are lax, free and capable of infinite development"[46] – in contrast with the rigidity that will be the hallmark of the following stages.

"The second stage, which we may call the *typal*, is predominantly psychological and ethical; all else, even the spiritual and religious, is subordinate to the psychological idea and to the ethical ideal which expresses it. Religion becomes then a mystic sanction for the ethical motive and discipline, *Dharma;* that becomes its chief social utility, and for the rest it takes a more and more otherworldly turn. The idea of the direct expression of the divine Being or cosmic Principle in man ceases to dominate or to be the leader and in the forefront; it recedes, stands in the background and finally disappears from the practice and in the end even from the theory of life.

"This typal stage creates the great social ideals which remain impressed upon the human mind even when the stage itself is passed. The principal active contribution it leaves behind when it is dead is the idea of social honour"[47] – the honour of the *brahmin* (the priest and man of knowledge), the *kshatriya* (the knight and ruler), the *vaishya* (the man of exchange and commerce) and the *shudra* (the worker and servant). Although the four castes are here denominated by their Sanskrit names, they have had their exact counterparts in the West.

The third, conventional stage of human society "is born when the external supports, the outward expressions of the spirit or the ideal, become more important than the ideal, the body or even the clothes more important than the person. Thus in the evolution of caste, the outward supports of the ethical fourfold order, – birth, economic function, religious ritual and sacrament, family custom, – each began to exaggerate enormously

---

46. Id., pp. 7 and 10.
47. Id., p. 11 (emphasis added).

31

its proportions and its importance in the scheme. At first, birth does not seem to have been of the first importance in the social order, for faculty and capacity prevailed; but afterwards, as the type fixed itself, its maintenance by education and tradition became necessary and education and tradition naturally fixed themselves in a hereditary groove ... Birth, family custom and remnants, deformations, new accretions of meaningless or fanciful religious sign and ritual, the very scarecrow and caricature of the old profound symbolism, became the riveting links of the system of caste in the iron age of the old society."[48]

"Then there arrives a period when the gulf between the convention and the truth becomes intolerable and the men of intellectual power arise, the great 'swallowers of formulas', who, rejecting robustly or fiercely or with the calm light of reason, symbol and type and convention, strike at the walls of the prison-house and seek by the individual reasonal moral sense or emotional desire the Truth that society has lost or buried in its white sepulchres. It is then that the individualistic age of religion and thought and society is created; the Age of Protestantism has begun, the Age of Reason, the Age of Revolt, Progress, Freedom. A partial and external freedom, still betrayed by the conventional age that preceded it into the idea that the Truth can be found in outsides, dreaming vainly that perfection can be determined by machinery, but still a necessary passage to the subjective period of humanity through which man has to circle back towards the recovery of his deeper self and a new upward line or a new revolving cycle of civilisation."[49]

"The inherent aim and effort and justification, the psychological seed-cause, the whole tendency of development of an individualistic age of mankind, all go back to the one dominant need of rediscovering the substantial truths of life, thought and action which have been overlaid by the falsehood of conventional standards no longer alive to the truth of the ideas from which their conventions started." However, "the need of

---

48. Id., pp. 11 and 12.
49. Id., p. 14.

a developing humanity is not to return always to its old ideas. Its need is to progress to a larger fulfilment in which, if the old is at all taken up, it must be transformed and exceeded. For the underlying truth of things is constant and eternal, but its mental figures, its life forms, its physical embodiments call constantly for growth and change ..."

"The individualistic age is, then, a radical attempt of mankind to discover the truth and law both of the individual being and of the world to which the individual belongs. It may begin, as it began in Europe, with the endeavour to get back, more especially in the sphere of religion, to the original truth which convention has overlaid, defaced and distorted; but from that first step it must proceed to others and in the end to a general questioning of the foundations of thought and practice in all the spheres of human life and action. A revolutionary reconstruction of religion, philosophy, science, art and society is the last inevitable outcome. It proceeds at first by the light of the individual mind and reason, by its demand on life and its experience of life; but it must go from the individual to the universal. For the effort of the individual soon shows him that he cannot securely discover the truth and law of his own being without discovering some universal law and truth to which he can relate it. Of the universe he is a part; in all but his deepest spirit he is its subject, a small cell in that tremendous organic mass: his substance is drawn from its substance and by the law of its life the law of his life is determined and governed. From a new view and knowledge of the world must proceed his new view and knowledge of himself, of his power and capacity and limitations, of his claim on existence and the high road and the distant or immediate goal of his individual and social destiny."[50]

"... In his study of himself and the world [man] cannot but come face to face with the soul in himself and the soul in the world and find it to be an entity so profound, so complex, so full of hidden secrets and powers that his intellectual reason betrays itself as an insufficient light and a fumbling seeker: it is

---

50. Id., pp. 27 ff.

successfully analytical only of superficialities and of what lies just behind the superficies. The need of a deeper knowledge must then turn him to the discovery of new powers and means within himself ... All these tendencies, though in a crude, initial and ill-developed form, are manifest now in the world and are growing from day to day with a significant rapidity. And their emergence and greater dominance means the transition from the rationalistic and utilitarian period of human development which individualism has created to a greater *subjective* age of society. The change began by a rapid turning of the current of thought into large and profound movements contradictory of the old intellectual standards, a swift breaking of the old tables. The materialism of the nineteenth century gave place first to a novel and profound vitalism which has taken various forms from Nietzsche's theory of the Will to be and Will to Power as the root and law of life to the new pluralistic and pragmatic philosophy ...

"These tendencies of thought, which had until yesterday a profound influence on the life and thought of Europe prior to the outbreak of the Great War, especially in France[51] and Germany, were not a mere superficial recoil from intellectualism to life and action, – although in their application by lesser minds they often assumed that aspect; they were an attempt to read profoundly and live by the Life-Soul of the universe and tended to be deeply psychological and subjective in their method. From behind them, arising in the void created by the discrediting of the old rationalistic intellectualism, there has begun to arise a new Intuitionalism, not yet clearly aware of its own drive and nature, which seeks through the forms and powers of Life for that which is behind Life and sometimes even lays as yet uncertain hands on the sealed doors of the Spirit."[52]

Sri Aurobindo wrote this in 1927 when revising *The Human*

---

51. This remark remained valid long after the Great War (i.e. the First World War), considering Bergson's influence on Jean-Paul Sartre (see Bernard-Henri Lévy: *Le Siècle de Sartre*) and Nietzsche's influence on Michel Foucault and others.
52. Sri Aurobindo: *The Human Cycle*, p. 30.

*Cycle.* To his inner eye the line of development was distinctly discernible, and his vision would be confirmed by its realisation – as can be read in his and the Mother's biographies and partly in the following chapters of this book. But the working out of this line of development had to be done in spite of the terrible resistance of the opposing forces resulting in a clash, or rather a series of clashes; and whether it would succeed or fail could not be foreseen at the time. There came, for instance, the direct attack on Sri Aurobindo when he broke his thigh; there came the outbreak of the Second World War, of which the real causes and implications are not yet understood by the historians; and there came the necessity of his conscious and voluntary descent into death – all of this, and much more, a saga worthy of the unwinding of the cycles and their arrival at "the giant point" of the turn into "the subjective age".

One should not be misled by the word "subjective", which may be seen as rather narrow considering the unimaginably large development it indicates. The subjective age represents everything Sri Aurobindo and the Mother foresaw for the future. The twentieth century has been branded the cruellest, most absurd period in history ever. Certainly, cruelty and apparent absurdity were among its main characteristics, but its true significance may prove to be quite different.

# 2
# The Avataric Field

> *Surely, for the earth-consciousness the very fact that the Divine manifests himself is the greatest of all splendours. Consider the obscurity here and what it would be if the Divine did not directly intervene and the Light of Lights did not break out of the obscurity – for that is the meaning of the [avataric] manifestation.*[1]
>
> – SRI AUROBINDO

The concept of the "Avatar" is generally understood to be typically Hindu, although, under other names, it is also alive in the West as a designation of Jesus Christ. While in Hinduism there is a succession of Avatars throughout the evolution, in Christianity Christ is supposed to be the one and only Avatar. In this, Christianity has been very "Eurocentric" and circumscribed in its outlook. The excuse is that Christian theology was embedded within a historical horizon beyond which it could not see or reach for many centuries.

In Hinduism, the fact that the Avatar incarnates at times of evolutionary crises to put matters straight is better known than the fact that he also comes when a special work of evolutionary development is to be done. The reason is Sri Krishna's well-known pronouncement in the *Bhagavad Gita:* "Whensoever there is the fading of the Dharma and the uprising of unrighteousness, then I loose myself forth into birth."[2] Of course, both reasons for the Avatar's embodiment upon Earth are not exclusive of each other: the special reason for the coming may well be part and even the cause of an evolutionary crisis – as

---
1. Sri Aurobindo: *Letters on Yoga,* p. 401.
2. *Bhagavad Gita,* IV. 7 (Sri Aurobindo's translation).

## 2. The Avataric Field

was the case in the coming of Sri Aurobindo and the Mother, a double-poled, male-female, complete Avatar for the first time in the history of humanity.

According to Sri Aurobindo's definition: "An Avatar, roughly speaking, is one who is conscious of the presence and power of the Divine born in him or descended into him and governing from within his will and life and action; he feels identified inwardly with this divine power and presence."[3] In India it is known that there are also other beings in a human incarnation who are charged with a special divine mission, and who are called *vibhutis*. "A Vibhuti", writes Sri Aurobindo, "is supposed to embody some power of the Divine and is enabled by it to act with great force in the world, but that is all that is necessary to make him a Vibhuti: the power may be very great, but the consciousness is not that of an inborn or indwelling Divinity. This is the distinction we can gather from the Gita which is the main authority on this subject."[4]

Among the Vibhutis may be counted: Veda Vyasa, Hatshepsut, Moses, Pericles, Socrates, Alexander, Confucius, Lao Tse, Julius Caesar, Caesar Augustus, Mohammed, Joan of Arc, Leonardo da Vinci, Napoleon, Shankara, Ramakrishna, Vivekananda, and undoubtedly many more in all times and climes. All of them were concretely aware that they had a specific, superhuman mission to fulfil and so they did. It should be noted that some of them were atheists, like Julius Gaius Caesar. Secondly, morality seems not to be a criterion. "All morality is a convention", said Sri Aurobindo, and conventions are not binding on divinely empowered actors and acts. Thirdly, many Vibhutis, like the Avatars, left an imprint on the memory of the species (which often is also true of the presence of their counterparts, the incarnations or emanations of the great Asuras), although others may have done their work in obscurity and remained unknown.

Turning back to the concept of the Avatar, a few quotations

---
3. Sri Aurobindo: *Letters on Yoga*, p. 406.
4. Ibid.

from Sri Aurobindo's letters may complete our understanding of it.

- "There are two sides of the phenomenon of Avatarhood, the Divine Consciousness and the instrumental personality. The Divine Consciousness is omnipotent but it has put forth the instrumental personality in Nature under the conditions of Nature and it uses it according to the rules of the game – though also sometimes to change the rules of the game. If Avatarhood is only a flashing miracle, then I have no use for it. If it is a coherent part of the arrangement of the omnipotent Divine in Nature, then I can understand and accept it."[5]

- "An Avatar is not at all bound to be a spiritual prophet – he is never in fact merely a prophet, he is a realiser, an establisher – not of outward things only, though he does realise something in the outward also, but, as I have said, of something essential and radical needed for the terrestrial evolution which is the evolution of the embodied spirit through successive stages towards the Divine."[6]

- "I have said that the Avatar is one who comes to open the Way for humanity to a higher consciousness – if nobody can follow the way, then either our conception of the thing, which is also that of Christ and Krishna and Buddha also, is all wrong or the whole life and action of the Avatar is quite futile. X seems to say that there is no way and no possibility of following, that the struggles and sufferings of the Avatar are unreal and all humbug – there is no possibility of struggle for one who represents the Divine. Such a conception makes nonsense of the whole idea of Avatarhood; there is then no reason for it, no necessity in it, no meaning in it. The Divine being all-powerful can lift people up without bothering to come down on earth. It is only if it is a part of the world-arrangement that he should take upon himself the

---
5. Id., p. 408.
6. Id., p. 415.

## 2. The Avataric Field

burden of humanity and open the Way that Avatarhood has any meaning."[7]

- "The Avatar is not supposed to act in a non-human way – he takes up human action and uses human methods with the human consciousness in front and the Divine behind. If he did not his taking a human body would have no meaning and would be of no use to anybody. He could just as well have stayed above and done things from there."[8]

- "An Avatar or Vibhuti have the knowledge that is necessary for their work, they need not have more. There was absolutely no reason why Buddha should know what was going on in Rome. An Avatar even does not manifest all the Divine omniscience and omnipotence; he has not come for any such unnecessary display; all that is behind him but not in the front of his consciousness. As for the Vibhuti, the Vibhuti need not even know that he is a power of the Divine. Some Vibhutis like Julius Caesar for instance have been atheists. Buddha himself did not believe in a personal God, only in some impersonal and indescribable Permanent."[9]

- "Because he [i.e. the Avatar] chooses to limit or determine his action by conditions, it does not make him less omnipotent. His self-limitation is itself an act of omnipotence … Certain conditions have been established for the game and so long as those conditions remain unchanged certain things are not done, – so we say they are impossible, can't be done.

- If the conditions are changed then the same things are done or at least become licit – allowable, legal according to the so-called laws of Nature, and then we say they can be done. The Divine also acts according to the conditions of the game. He may change them but he has to change them first,

---
7. Id., p. 408.
8. Id., p. 409.
9. Ibid.

not proceed, while maintaining the conditions, to act by a series of miracles."[10]

- "The Avatar is not bound to do extraordinary actions, but he is bound to give his acts or his work or what he is – any of this or all – a significance and an effective power that are part of something to be done in the history of the earth and its races."[11]

- "It is not by your mind that you can hope to understand the Divine and its action, but by the growth of a true and divine consciousness within you. If the Divine were to unveil and reveal itself in all its glory, the mind might feel a Presence, but it would not understand its action or its nature. It is in the measure of your own realisation and by the birth and growth of the greater consciousness in yourself that you will see the Divine and understand its action even behind its terrestrial disguises."[12]

As the incarnation of an Avatar is a direct divine intervention in the evolution, it must be planned and timed "from behind the veil", from the heart of Eternity, so that it comes at the right moment and has the intended effect on the stage of our evolutionary manifestation. The action of an Avatar consists of four phases: the time of his advent; his presence on Earth; the period after his passing, when apparently nothing or very little of his work is patently perceptible; and the time of accomplishment, when the results of his mission are a concrete part of the manifestation. These are the four phases of the avataric action which can be seen as one new field, a spiritual force field, bringing about the creation of a new step in the evolution or whatever may be the mission of the Avatar. We will now briefly sketch these four phases as applied to the work of Sri Aurobindo and the Mother.

---

10. Id., p. 411.
11. Id., p. 414.
12. Id., p. 410.

## First Phase: The Advent of the Avatar

Sri Aurobindo was born in 1872 and the Mother in 1878. It is becoming fashionable among historians to write about "the long 19th century" (from the French Revolution till 1914, the beginning of the First World War) and "the short 20th century" (from 1914 till 1989, the collapse of the Communist Bloc). It might be much more appropriate to see the 20th century up to 1989 as a whole, intimately connected with the last decades of the 19th century. For there was doubtlessly a complex historical period preceding up to the First World War. It is therefore justifiable to consider the 19th century as beginning with the French Revolution and ending with the collapse of the ideological foundations of the bourgeoisie in the last decades of the 19th century, a process directly connected with the outbreak of the First World War.

The last decades of the 19th century were the time of "the second industrial revolution". The first industrial revolution had been powered by coal and steel, this new phase of industrial development was powered by oil and electricity. The inventions made at that time are still with us in one form or another: the bicycle ("that most beneficent of all the period's machines"), the motor car with its internal combustion engine, the telephone, the telegraph, the gramophone, the cinematic camera, the electric generator, the light bulb, etc.

One result of the new, ever-accelerating industrial development was a sudden increase of workers in the cities. Their living and working conditions were terrible; this problem reached such dimensions that it must either be solved or explode into widespread revolution. This was the time of the rise of socialism, which in its various forms referred back to the theories of Karl Marx and Friedrich Engels. It was also the time of many utopian social systems and of militant anarchism.

Marx was only one of the thinkers directly influencing the age; the other principal ones were Charles Darwin, Friedrich Nietzsche and Sigmund Freud. Darwin gave a severe blow to the image man had of himself as the king of creation. Nietzsche, "the eloquent and menacing prophet of an impending catastrophe", proclaimed the end of the Western civilisation based on Christianity; Freud showed that the psychology of the human being is much more complex than either the Greeks or the Christians had thought or dared to think. "The crisis of reason is most obvious in psychology, at least insofar as it tried to come to terms not with experimental situations, but with the human mind as a whole. What remained of the solid citizen pursuing rational aims by maximising personal utilities, if his pursuit was based on a bundle of 'instincts' like those of animal, if the rational mind was only a boat tossed on the waves and currents of the unconscious, or even if rational consciousness was only a special kind of consciousness 'whilst all about it, parted from it by the flimsiest of screens, there lie potential forms of consciousness entirely different'?"[13]

What was actually going on, generally speaking, was that the idea of "reality" was radically put into question, in the first place the reality constituting the human being itself. Since the Renaissance, the firmly fixed foundations of the medieval world view had been gradually eroded, to such an extent that the bourgeois 19th century had been living in a hollow and very vulnerable reality; still it had to hold up appearances, and it is therefore generally branded as hypocritical and fake. The Impressionists were the first who could no longer stand the bourgeois artificiality – Manet's *Le Déjeuner sur l'herbe* dates from 1863 – and created forms of expression of the authentic artistic experience. Their revolution was not based on any philosophical thought or intention; it sprang directly from a need of the heart. (The impressionists, however bourgeois in part of their personality, may be considered as the forerunners or the first wave of what Sri Aurobindo called "the subjective age".)

A new scientific paradigm originated simultaneously with the artistic revolution. "Every historian is struck by the fact that the revolutionary transformation of the scientific world view in these years forms part of a more general, and dramatic,

---

13. Eric Hobsbawm: *The Age of Empire*, p. 271.

abandonment of established and often long-accepted values, truths and ways of looking at the world ... It may be pure accident or arbitrary selection that Planck's quantum theory, the rediscovery of Mendel, Husserl's *Logische Untersuchungen*, Freud's *Interpretation of Dreams* and Cézanne's *Still Life with Onions* can all be dated to 1900 ... but the coincidence of dramatic innovation in several fields remains striking."[14]

All this happened mainly in the West while the East, in Sri Aurobindo's words, was asleep. But not for long. For the decades we are considering also saw the culmination of colonialism. To many now "colonialism" is a dirty word; yet it was colonialism that prepared the world to become one, and this unification, as we will see, constituted an important element in the evolution of humanity. "It is a surprising fact that in most parts of Africa the entire experience of colonialism from original occupation to the formation of independent states, fits within a single lifetime – say that of Winston Churchill (1874-1965)."[15]

In those years the political situation grew enormously complicated and confused. The power game was in full swing and could erupt into war at any time, though nobody was able to foretell among whom exactly, let alone what might be the outcome. Kings, queens and other scions of the feudal nobility that had been ruling over Europe since Charlemagne were still on their thrones, a century after the French Revolution and Napoleon, but it was generally felt that most of them were colossi with clay feet and could topple over at any moment. The historians agree that the overall situation at the turn of the 19th into the 20th century was incredibly tense for reasons nobody could explain.

When in 1914 war finally happened, it was greeted with relief, and even joy and enthusiasm, by the participants, ignorant of the fact that so many young people would be slaughtered. Documentaries of festive crowds filmed at that time are still there for us to view. To quote Hobsbawm a last time: "As bourgeois

---
14. Id., p. 256.
15. Id., p. 79.

Europe moved in growing material comfort towards its catastrophe, we observe the curious phenomenon of a bourgeoisie, or at least a significant part of its youth and its intellectuals, which plunged willingly, even enthusiastically, into the abyss. Everyone knows of the young men ... who hailed the outbreak of the First World War like people who have fallen in love."[16] A striking testimony to these words are Rupert Brooke's lines, quoted in *Voices of the Great War:*

> Now, God be thanked Who has matched us with His hour,
> And caught our youth, and wakened us from sleeping,
> With hand made sure, clear eye, and sharpened power,
> To turn, as swimmers into cleanness leaping,
> Glad from a world grown old and cold and weary,
> Leave the sick hearts that honour could not move ...

From the Aurobindonian perspective it may be justified to ascribe the tension, the almost unbearable pressure at the time, to the fact that humanity was preparing for the greatest change in its history – a change that would make the 20th century the most eventful and as yet least understood century. It would be "the most revolutionary [period] ever experienced by the human race". Fundamentally, the whole tense situation was created for and by the coming of the Avatar; it was created by the pressure of the avataric field.

## Second Phase: The Presence of the Avatar

The Avatar is born in the circumstances determined by his divine self from outside the manifestation; these circumstances are chosen to make the execution of his mission possible. Born from humans in a human body, the Avatar's first years are a time of self-discovery. Generally speaking, he is from an early

---
16. Id., p. 190.

## 2. The Avataric Field

age aware of a special destiny and mission in life, although not yet of his divinity. But this was not the case with the Buddha, who seems to have led a normal princely life up to the moment of his great discovery. When Sri Aurobindo was a boy and reading about the freedom movements in Ireland and Italy, he felt strongly that he had a role to play in the liberation of his motherland, but nothing more.

Sri Aurobindo has explicitly stated that his and the Mother's consciousness were one. This is indirectly shown by the parallelism of their early lives at a time they did not yet know of each other, at least not in their surface awareness. Both had parents who wanted their children to become the best in the world; the parents of both were atheists; both were atheists themselves in their youth; their first contact with yoga took place in 1905, the year Sri Aurobindo started practising pranayama and the Mother discovered *La Revue cosmique*; both began their real yoga in 1908; both were instructed in an occult way by invisible teachers; the *Bhagavad Gita* played an important role in the development of both; Sri Aurobindo's *Record of Yoga* and the Mother's *Prayers and Meditations* were started at the same time; both discovered the Supermind and their mission independently ...

The earthly presence of the Avatar of the Supermind, Sri Aurobindo and the Mother, is better known than the life of any other Avatar. It should be understood, however, that our knowledge of them, however extensive, is only the tip of the iceberg, sufficient to construct a limited notion of who they were through convergence of the known facts. What does it mean, for example, to have the God Krishna living in one's own body, as from 1926 till 1950 he was living in Sri Aurobindo's? What was the splendid overmental world the Mother created in 1927? The reports of the disciples then present and actually involved in it hardly provide us with anything concrete. Which other interventions by Sri Aurobindo and the Mother were there in the Second World War apart from the few they mentioned? Why did Sri Aurobindo have to descend into death? What did the Mother actually mean when she said, in the last years, that her body was only a means to render an external contact with her possible? ...

The life of the Avatar has always a direct interaction with the life of humanity, for such is its *raison d'être*. It is the task of the Vibhuti to solve particular, localised problems, but it is the task of the Avatar to take the evolution forward at a point where even the most evolved terrestrial elements are no longer capable of doing so. This is the explanation of the fact that the Avatar, according to Krishna in the *Gita,* incarnates at times of crisis. The crisis necessitates the coming of the Avatar, as well as his coming causes the crisis. Rama, the Avatar of the rational mind, fought his great battle with the ten-headed asura Ravana, king of Lanka.[17] Krishna incarnated at the time of the Mahabharata war, when the world of the peoples who participated in that war was in peril of perdition because of the Kauravas. The Buddha came at the time of the calcification of the Vedic ritual; so important was the new spiritual impetus he caused that it spread through a whole continent and continues working in the present day, when there are more than 500 million Buddhists. Christ appeared in a Mediterranean world in upheaval, at least as bewildering to the people then as is our turbulent world to us now. The Twentieth Century is the history of the interaction of Sri Aurobindo and the Mother's Yoga with humanity.

Yet, despite their profound, decisive influence, the Avatars are usually not recognised. "I suppose very few recognised him [Krishna] as an Avatar,"[18] wrote Sri Aurobindo. The same could be said of Buddha, regarded as a demon by the brahmans, and Christ, who was crucified as a criminal. The same could be said of Sri Aurobindo and the Mother, who still are practically unknown. The followers recognising them as the Avatar number no more than a handful, and even among them the recognition

---

17. See Sri Aurobindo's *Letters on Yoga,* pp. 414 ff. "As for the Avatarhood, I accept it for Rama because he fills a place in the scheme – and seems to me to fill it rightly – and because when I read the Ramayana I feel a great afflatus which I recognise and which makes of its story – a mere faery-tale though it seems – a parable of a great critical transitional event that happened in the terrestrial evolution ..."
18. Sri Aurobindo: *Letters on Yoga,* p. 406.

## 2. The Avataric Field

was and is not unanimous. A disciple to whom Sri Aurobindo once wrote "I have cherished you like a friend and a son" never recognised him as an Avatar but only as his guru, while he kept his distance from the Mother. For those who follow a certain yogic approach, for instance of devotion, to recognise, them as the Avatar may not be necessary because, if their attitude is faithful, the recognition will be given to them at the time of the fulfilment of their *sadhana*. But how can one have any idea of the importance of Sri Aurobindo and the Mother's Work if one remains ignorant of their avataric function and does not perceive them as such?

Speaking of followers and disciples: the Avatar never comes alone; he always surrounds himself with individuals, incarnated souls, who represent the whole of humanity so that, through them, he may touch the complete field of his action. As Sri Aurobindo wrote: "Some psychic beings have come here [near him in Pondicherry] who are ready to join with great lines of consciousness above, represented often by beings of the higher planes and are therefore specially fitted to join with the Mother intimately in the great work that has to be done. These have all a special relation with the Mother which adds to the past one."[19] He also wrote: "A number of souls have been sent to see that it shall be now."[20] The Buddha had his circle of disciples, devotees and followers; so had Krishna (the Pandavas and their allies) and so had Christ.

"No individual realisation can be complete or even come near to this perfection", said the Mother to her audience at the Ashram Playground, "if it is not in harmony with at least a group of consciousnesses representative of a new world. There is, in spite of everything, so great an interdependence between the individual and the collectivity that the individual realisation ... is limited, diminished by the irresponsive atmosphere – if I may put it like that – of what surrounds it. And it is certain that the entire terrestrial life has to follow a certain line of progress,

---

19. Sri Aurobindo: *On the Mother*, p. 168.
20. Sri Aurobindo: *On Himself*, p. 368.

so that a new world and a new consciousness may manifest. And this is why I said at the beginning that it depends at least partially on you."[21]

Touching again upon this subject shortly afterwards she said: "The personal realisation has no limits. One can become inwardly, in oneself, perfect and infinite. But the outer realisation is necessarily limited, and if one wants to exert a general action, at least a minimum number of physical beings are needed. In a very old tradition it was said that twelve were enough, but in the complexities of modern life this does not seem possible. There must be a representative group. You know nothing about it, or you are not very much aware of it, but each one of you represents one of the difficulties that must be conquered for the transformation, and this makes quite a number of difficulties! I have written somewhere ... that more than a difficulty, each one represents an *impossibility* to be solved. And it is the whole of all these impossibilities that can be transformed into the Work, the Realisation. Each case is an impossibility to be solved, and it is when all these impossibilities will be solved that the Work will be accomplished."[22]

Some of the most prominent disciples of the Avatars have been elevated in the esteem of the faithful to a quasi-divine status, a status they surely did not enjoy in their lifetime. For as their Master remained unrecognised by the multitude, so were they. "Those who were with Krishna were in all appearance men like other men", wrote Sri Aurobindo. "They spoke and acted with each other as men with men and were not thought of by those around them as gods."[23] As far as the disciples who were with Sri Aurobindo and the Mother are concerned, telling anecdotes illustrating the last quotation can be found abundantly in Sri Aurobindo's correspondence. The disciples of Christ just fled away at the moment of his highest need.

Still, whatever the shortcomings of their outer personality – in the Yoga the most difficult part to change – there is no doubt

---

21. The Mother: *Questions and Answers 1955*, pp. 323-24.
22. Id., p. 415 (emphasis added).
23. Sri Aurobindo: *Letters on Yoga*, p. 406.

## 2. The Avataric Field

that the companions of the Avatar are always very special human incarnations. From the texts left us by Sri Aurobindo and the Mother we know that their disciples had participated in their avataric and vibhutic mission in times past. The Mother even said so explicitly to her audience of the *Questions and Answers*. They belonged, she said, to "the family of the aspiration", and she had promised most of them in a previous incarnation that they would be present at the time of the great realisation, meaning the descent of the Supermind. It should nevertheless be kept in mind that the evolution proceeds through "the clash of opposites", as Sri Aurobindo put it, through the clash of the forces for and against the divine design. (The Asuras were, after all, the "first-born" and the Gods the "second-born".) Therefore he and the Mother also took some of the most powerful embodiments of the evolutionary resistance into their proximity, in order to work directly upon them and through them upon the whole of humanity. (The Asura and Rakshasa are there in all of us.) All were her children, the Mother said, the *anshas*[24] of the Gods as well as the *anshas* of the Asuras, and the conversion of the latter formed an essential part in the movement of transition towards the New World.

For those who want to see, or are chosen to see, the lives of Sri Aurobindo and the Mother are a continuous confirmation of the veracity of their avatarhood; they have also confirmed it on many occasions, in most cases confidentially. And the portent of the present times is such that something of prime importance must be happening in the development of humanity; the crisis that humanity and its *bhumi*, the Earth, are undergoing is on a scale which requires the intervention of an Avatar. If all this is true, then the Avatar has been present on the Earth in the Twentieth Century. Then Kalki, with the sword of Truth, has fought his battles, even though his physical incarnation was not as described in the Puranas. The World-Redeemer came, and nobody recognised him – as is humanity's wont.

---

24. Every soul is part (*ansha*) of a God, who is a direct power or emanation of the Divine. As the Asuras too have their (countless) emanations, the word *ansha* might also be used, even if metaphorically, in relation with them.

## Third Phase: After the Departure of the Avatar

Then comes the time when the Avatar leaves his body and the disciples stay behind, bereft of the sun of their lives, perplexed, stunned. They may be ridiculed by others for their belief in a person who promised them so much – a wonderful new life or the means to realise it – and who seemingly left them with so little after having died like any other mortal. The Buddha did not write a single word and neither did Christ, except for some mysterious words or signs in the sand. Moreover, in the case of the latter his return in glory was expected within the lifetime of those who had been with him, but they waited in vain.

Sri Aurobindo, who was supposed to be immortal according to many of his disciples and followers, left his body in December 1950; the Mother, after years of what looked like physical deterioration and illness, left her body in November 1973. Both times the bewilderment in the Aurobindonian community was widespread and the faith of many deeply shaken.

It is in this third phase that some harrowing questions crop up. What about the expectation that Sri Aurobindo and the Mother would stay on Earth forever? (They have never said so.) What about the appearance of the immortal supramental beings and the New World? (What Sri Aurobindo and the Mother said about the transitional being was not taken into consideration till the present day.) Would Sri Aurobindo and/or the Mother come back, preferably as soon as possible? (Since 1973 several women have declared themselves to be an incarnation of the Mother.) Are there any signs that the Work is going on, that the Supermind is active? (The fact of the presence of the Consciousness of the Overman is seldom, if ever, referred to.) In short, was it true what Sri Aurobindo and the Mother had written or said, or was it another grandiose effort ending with the traditional "fiasco"?

These questions are rarely formulated in public or in writing. Some disciples and followers have bypassed the mental problematics, taken the devotional attitude, and included Sri Aurobindo and the Mother in the pantheon of the Gods whom they adore. In many the devotion is sincere and the support if not the reason of their whole life. And there are the ones who have kept a living relation with the Great Beings they once saw embodied before their eyes. Time goes by and the world changes.

The third phase of the avataric intervention in the world may well be the most trying phase for those involved in it. The Avatar is no longer there in the body to be seen or to be asked for his/her advice and personal support. The new teaching is interpreted in many ways and often distorted or appropriated by egos who consider themselves advanced on the path, or the sole heirs to it, or gifted with the exclusivity of a correct understanding. Verbal altercations and personal or group enmities arise because the teaching has to be interpreted in order to adapt it to new situations in a changing world. There are power struggles among the believers, hidden or overt.

The third phase covers the span of time – decades? centuries? – in which each and every embodied soul called to participate in the avataric Work has to fend for itself, with as its only support the staff of Faith and the inner development. Most often the disciples who were the companions of the Avatar are held in high esteem and some of them may gradually acquire superhuman proportions in the minds of those left behind. Their contribution to the Work was considerable, for sure. But the contribution to the Work of the souls that chose to be the vanguard of humanity in the most trying phase, when the Avatar is no longer there and the result of his Work is not yet concretely perceptible, is no less considerable.

## *Fourth Phase: The Fulfilment of the Avataric Mission*

Finally, there is the time of accomplishment, for no Avatar incarnates without the divine certitude that his Work will be consummated. This certitude is the seal on his Work. The divine Vision saw the necessity of the coming and planned the means, time and required circumstances for it. The divine Power performed the Yoga, the realisation of something impossible and totally new in the evolution of the Earth. On the basis built by the Avatar, his divine Self sees to it, after his departure from the physical scene, that the Work develops and grows to maturity. Only his Self from behind the veil can have the necessary Vision and Knowledge of a future that seems totally utopian and unreal at the time the foundations of the new element in the evolution are realised. The Avatar remains present on Earth in an occult way at least till this Work is done and keeps intervening in the earthly circumstances to bring it about. The dimensions of his mission cannot be completed within the short span of a human life. The fourth phase of the fulfilment is an integral part of "the avataric field".

This may seem a matter of belief. A look back at the avataric mission of the Buddha and Christ, however, provides concrete evidence. At the time the Buddha left his body, little seemed to be left of his superhuman effort except the presence of some followers in a corner of what is now the Indian state of Bihar. The subsequent development of Buddhism and its branching out in many variations and directions is impressive. In its heyday, Buddhism in one form or other covered most of the Asian continent and became the faith and the way of life of millions of people; it simultaneously created a literature which is one of the treasures of mankind. When Christ died abandoned on the cross nothing seemed to be left of all that he had preached and tried to inculcate in his disciples, followers and the crowds that had assembled to listen to him. Centuries later the European civilisation came into existence from the seeds he had sown in the human soil. ("Christ from his cross humanised Europe", wrote Sri Aurobindo in one of his aphorisms.) Today the West still considers him the paragon of all that is good and noble in the human being, and his followers number seven or eight hundred million.

When will there be a concrete result of Sri Aurobindo and the Mother's Yoga, in other words, when will the first signs of a supramental transformation be perceptible to ordinary humans?

## 2. The Avataric Field

This question was considered of secondary importance during Sri Aurobindo's lifetime. What counted then – "the one thing needful" – was the descent of the Supermind, as Sri Aurobindo told Nirodbaran in their correspondence; *that* should be the aim of the whole effort and all the rest was premature speculation.[25] (The manifestation of the Supermind took place in 1956.)

About the actual supramental transformation Sri Aurobindo at first talked vaguely in terms of thousands of years, and observed that this would be a very short time considering the scope of the evolutionary transformation envisaged. Towards the end of his life his guess was, according to the Mother, about three hundred years. In 1956, the Mother's own estimation was still "a certain number of a thousand years" and "some centuries". Between 1958 and 1973 she often repeated Sri Aurobindo's estimation of "at least three hundred years", considering this the minimum time required. Towards the end she usually referred to Sri Aurobindo's estimation of "three hundred years".

All the same, let us not forget that before another three centuries have passed, some unpredictable, very fundamental and apparently miraculous changes will take place leading up to the appearance of a supramental being whose presence we, ordinary mortals, could not even endure. For the Supermind is at work and so is the Overman Consciousness. No doubt, the future has always been unpredictable to the human being, unable to "even see the step ahead."[26] The characteristics of the radical events ahead, however, should be identifiable as the conditions necessary for the appearance of the supramental being: world-unity in diversity; supercession of the ego in individuals, communities, religions, peoples and nations; fulfilment of the highest capabilities of the human being leading towards the realisation of his most sublime ideals; physical acquisitions pointing towards a body with the capacities of the superman;

---

25. See Nirodbaran: *Correspondence with Sri Aurobindo*, p. 673.
26. "All history is a series of miracles. It is very easy to explain *post facto* the ineluctability of the events; but if our systems of explanation were reliable, they would also provide us with the capacity to anticipate, yet, the events could not care less about our anticipations." (Leszek Kolakowski)

a universal empathy with all beings and with the universe as a precondition to the ultimate flowering of Love.

Words and thoughts like these were but seldom expressed in the countless messages on the threshold of the new millennium. Yet they are not completely foreign to us. They were abroad in the magic Sixties, peaking in '68, though soon stifled by a human mind in bewilderment by what overtook it; they were abroad in '89, when the Berlin Wall fell, pulling the Communist Bloc down with it. As Sri Aurobindo wrote in "The Hour of God": "This is the time of the unexpected."

# 3
# East and West[1]

> *To this mutual self-discovery and self-illumination by the fusion of the old Eastern and the new Western knowledge the thought of the world is already turning.*[2]
>
> – SRI AUROBINDO
>
> *The safety of Europe has to be sought in the recognition of the spiritual aim of human existence, otherwise she will be crushed by the weight of her own unillumined knowledge and soulless organisation.*[3]
>
> – SRI AUROBINDO

The significance of the time we are living in has been examined in the two previous chapters viewing the present "turning point" from the perspective of the cycles humanity has traversed, and by interpreting the present as the third phase in the mission and action of the Avatar of the Supermind. In this chapter another approach with the same end will be suggested by considering the intrinsic value of the Eastern and Western civilisations, and their eventual reciprocality.

---

1. In this chapter the concepts "East" and "West" are used as they are in the works of Sri Aurobindo: in their symbolical, spiritual sense, which remains valid underneath the developments in the last decades.
2. Sri Aurobindo: *The Life Divine*, p. 114.
3. Sri Aurobindo: *Essays in Philosophy and Yoga*, p. 143.

## The Western Way – Greece

The difference between East and West is essentially a difference of culture. Seen in this way, the "West" means the various aspects and developments of the European culture, generally thought to have originated in the city-states of ancient Greece. Although this view is still the common one, set forth in all philosophical and historical manuals and works of reference, it becomes more and more open to doubt as the Middle-Eastern and Egyptian roots of ancient Greece are uncovered or rediscovered.[4]

A few elementary facts will prove that this new assessment of the origins of Greek culture is indeed convincing. The people of the eastern Mediterranean were able seafarers even in prehistoric times; it must have been as easy for them to hop from island to island southwards, in the direction of the Egyptian delta, as it manifestly was eastwards, in the direction of what is now Turkey and the islands along its coast, which would become the first important centre of Greek culture and philosophy. Secondly, there must have been compelling reasons for a number of prominent Greeks to journey to the Land of the Two Kingdoms (Upper and Lower Egypt) – Solon, Pythagoras, Herodotus and Plato among them – and to stay there for long periods. The Egyptian influence is quite evident in their teachings and writings. For example, Egypt is where Plato got his story about Atlantis. Still more important: according to Herodotus, "the father of history", most of the Greek gods were the counterparts of the Egyptian gods. "In the Egyptian language", he writes, "Apollo is called Horus, Demeter Isis, Artemis Bubastis". Neith is identified with Athena, Osiris with Dionysus, Hathor with Aphrodite, Ammon with Zeus, and so on.[5]

In the present context more need not be said about this fascinating topic. Its importance will be clear because it erodes another foundation of the bulwark of "Eurocentrism" that

---

4. See e.g. Martin Barnal: *Black Athena,* and Christos C. Evangeliou: *The Hellenic Philosophy – between Europe, Asia and Africa.*
5. Jacqueline de Romilly: *Pourquoi la Grèce?* p. 119.

has limited for centuries the Western outlook on the other civilisations of the world. The revelation of the true roots of ancient Greece diminishes in no way its special distinction; on the contrary, it makes it more profoundly understandable and thereby enriches it. Few have been greater admirers of Greece than Sri Aurobindo, who was intimately familiar with its culture and civilisation, read and wrote classical Greek fluently, and produced brilliant pages of poetry and prose dedicated to it.[6] He wrote, for instance, in *The Ideal of Human Unity*: "The cultural and civic life of the Greek city, of which Athens was the supreme achievement, a life in which living itself was an education, where the poorest as well as the richest sat together in the theatre to see and judge the dramas of Sophocles and Euripides, and the Athenian trader and shopkeeper took part in the subtle philosophical conversations of Socrates, created for Europe not only its fundamental political types and ideals but practically all its basic forms of intellectual, philosophical, literary and artistic culture."[7]

The fact that concerns us here is the emergence of the rational mind in classical Greece. It was there that Western man fully became "the mental being", a term defined by Aristotle as follows: "What is naturally proper to every creature is the highest and pleasantest for him. And so, to man, this will be the life of Reason, since Reason is, in the highest sense, a man's self."[8] According to Sri Aurobindo, though, the rational mind is not the highest level of existence man has access to: it is his specific, characteristic level, the "typal" level of the universal manifestation which he incarnates in the evolution. The fact that from Aristotle onwards Western philosophy considered it to be the highest level limits its outlook even in the present times.

The transition from the mythological to the rational age in ancient Greece took place at the time of Pericles, in Greece's

---

6. See K.D. Sethna: *Sri Aurobindo and Greece*. Sri Aurobindo's unfinished epic *Ilion* and his essay *Heraclitus* are masterpieces.
7. Sri Aurobindo: *The Human Cycle,* p. 360.
8. Quoted in William Barrett: *Irrational Man*, p. 89.

Golden Age. The instruments of this transition were the sophists – Protagoras, Gorgias, Prodicos, Hippias, Critias, and others – who were much more influential than is generally supposed. "Truly speaking, one does not understand anything of the century of Pericles and 'the Greek miracle' if one does not have a clear idea of the nature and the portent of their influence", writes Jacqueline de Romilly.[9] The sophists, according to this expert on ancient Greece, were the ones who questioned all current norms and opinions. They not only taught oratory, the necessary art for prominence in the public life of the city: they were philosophers "in the true sense of the term", whose innovating views freed the spirit. They initiated "a veritable intellectual and moral revolution". Though Socrates did not take money for his teachings, he, the Vibhuti of the rational mind for the West, was after all a sophist and regarded as such by the Athenians.

Referring to the role of the sophists, Sri Aurobindo writes: "The mind and the intellect must develop to their fullness so that the spirituality of the race may rise securely upward upon a broad basis of the developed lower nature in man, the intelligent mental being. Therefore we see that the reason in its growth either does away with the distinct spiritual tendency for a time, as in ancient Greece ..."[10] The sophists were feared and loathed by the traditional, reactionary factions in Athens because they openly expressed their rational doubts about the irrationalities of the religion, the myths and the Gods. They were attacked in the public gatherings, and for his free thinking Socrates will finally pay with his life. Another point of importance is that the *tabula rasa* advocated by the sophists "allowed to construct, on new grounds, a new morality centred on man alone" (de Romilly). In other words, the humanism and individualism for which the culture of ancient Greece is so highly praised and which would run as a golden thread through the subsequent stages of the West originated with the sophists. It should however be stressed

---

9. Jacqueline de Romilly: *Les grands sophistes dans l'Athenes de Pericles*, p. 10.
10. Sri Aurobindo: *The Human Cycle*, p. 188.

## 3. East and West

that all this concerns the Western civilisation. The irreversible acquisition of the rational mind by humanity in Greece was of primary consequence for the West and for everything the West stood and still stands for. William Barrett, in his standard study of existentialism, *Irrational Man,* writes: "The momentousness of this emergence of reason can be gauged by setting Greece over against the comparably high civilisations of India and China. These latter had a great flowering of sages at a time close to that of the pre-Socratics in Greece; but neither in India nor in China was reason fully isolated and distinguished – that is, differentiated – from the rest of man's psychic being, from his feeling and intuition. Oriental man remains intuitive, not rational."[11] This statement gives voice to a common Western misconception and shows Barrett's ignorance in the matter of the philosophical schools of ancient India and China, where the outflowering of rational thought preceded the classical period in Greece and was much more varied in its expressions.

The focus on the human being and the urge towards an individual evaluation of life are indisputably two of the great gifts the Greek civilisation bequeathed to the West. It seems justified to consider humanism (plus political democracy) and individualism as the foundations of "Europe", of the common culture which developed on the most western peninsula of the Eurasian landmass, spread to the Americas, and is now so influential worldwide. In a series of interviews Alison Browning had in 1989 with prominent European intellectuals these fundamentals were referred to time and again: "Europe equals humanism" (Eugene Ionesco); Europe stands for "a more human being" (Peter Härtling); Europe is "the land of the human ... the country of origin of the individual" (Denis de Rougemont).[12]

---

11. William Barrett: *Irrational Man*, p. 80.
12. *L'Europe et les intellectuels – Enquête internationale conduite par Alison Browning pour le Centre Européen de la Culture*, passim.

## Christianity

Another essential element that contributed to the building of European culture was Christianity. "Greece with its rational bent and its insufficient religious sense was unable to save its religion; it tended towards that sharp division between philosophy and science on one side and religion on the other which has been so peculiar a characteristic of the European mind", wrote Sri Aurobindo in his essay on *Heraclitus*.[13] "... Heraclitus prepares the way for the destruction of the old religion [by the sophists], the reign of pure philosophy and reason and *the void which was filled up by Christianity;* for man cannot live by reason alone ... Europe had killed its old creeds beyond revival and had to turn for its religion to Asia."[14] Jesus Christ was an Asian.

This may be the place to quote a revealing, seminal text of Sri Aurobindo's, which was published in the *Arya* in 1915 and covers the whole range of the relations between East and West. It goes as follows: "The fundamental difference [between East and West] has been that Asia has served predominantly (not exclusively) as a field for man's spiritual experience and progression, Europe has been rather a workshop for his mental and vital activities. As the cycle progressed, the Eastern continent has more and more converted itself into a storehouse of spiritual energy sometimes active and reaching forward to new development, sometimes conservative and quiescent. Three or four times in history a stream of this energy has poured out upon Europe, but each time Europe has rejected wholly or partially the spiritual substance of the afflatus and used it rather as an impulse to fresh intellectual and material activity and progress.

"The first attempt was the filtering of Egyptian, Chaldean and Indian wisdom through the thought of the Greek philosophers from Pythagoras to Plato and the Neo-Platonists; the result was the brilliantly intellectual and unspiritual civilisation of Greece and Rome. But it prepared the way for the second attempt *when*

---

13. Sri Aurobindo: *Heraclitus*, in *Essays in Philosophy and Yoga*, p. 247.
14. Id. pp. 247-48 (emphasis added).

## 3. East and West

*Buddhism and Vaishnavism filtered through the Semitic temperament entered Europe in the form of Christianity.* Christianity came within an ace of spiritualising and even asceticising the mind of Europe; it was baffled by its own theological deformation in the minds of the Greek fathers of the Church and by the sudden flooding of Europe with a German barbarism whose temperament in its merits no less than in its defects was the very anti-type of the Christian spirit and the Graeco-Roman intellect.

"The Islamic invasion of Spain and the southern coast of the Mediterranean – curious as the sole noteworthy example of Asiatic culture using the European method of material and political irruption as opposed to a peaceful invasion by ideas – may be regarded as a third attempt. The result of its meeting with Graecised Christianity was the reawakening of the European mind in feudal and Catholic Europe and the obscure beginnings of modern thought and science.

"The fourth and last attempt, which is as yet only in its slow initial stage is the quiet entry of Eastern and chiefly of Indian thought into Europe, first through the veil of German metaphysics, more latterly by its subtle influence in reawakening the Celtic, Scandinavian and Slavonic idealism, mysticism, religionism, and the direct and open penetration of Buddhism, Theosophy, Vedantism, Bahaism and other Oriental influences in both Europe and America."[15]

Christ, who according to Sri Aurobindo was influenced by Buddhism and Vaishnavism, brought the experience of the soul and therefore of individual spirituality to the Hebrews, the People of the Law. His legacy would be an important contribution to the development of individualism in the West. The soul is a part of the Divine – the Son of Man is also the Son of God. As each human being has a soul, Christ declared that he had come to show a new way to the whole of humanity, low as well as high. This doubly offended the Hebraic authorities; he was a blasphemer for asserting that he and all human beings had God within them and could communicate directly with Him, and he

---

15. Id. pp. 141-42 (emphasis added).

upset the social order by mixing with people who were no better than outcasts in Hebraic society. (The first Christian converts in the Empire were for the most part women and slaves.)

Nowadays it is generally known that Christ and the religions which claim descendence from him are two different things. Christianity was much more the creation of St. Paul and the Church Fathers than of Christ himself, although the shining core of Christ's mission has remained present on the Earth for a long time to contact with the soul and follow its true spiritual path, called *bhakti* by the Indians, devotional love. "To humanise Europe", as Sri Aurobindo put it, Christianity and the then still living force of its founder used the apparatus of the Roman Empire, which itself had absorbed the civilisation of the Greeks. Thus Greece, Rome, Judaism and Christianity became the pillars upon which Europe was built. All four elements have remained active through the ages and are still directly influential in what is now called Western civilisation.

## The Teutonic Lapse

History tells us how the Roman Empire in the fourth and fifth centuries gradually disintegrated under pressure from the barbarian tribes on its northern frontiers. "The old Hellenic or Graeco-Roman civilisation perished, among other reasons, because it only imperfectly generalised culture in its own society and was surrounded by huge masses of humanity who were still possessed by the barbarian habit of mind", writes Sri Aurobindo. "Civilisation can never be safe so long as, confining the cultured mentality to a small minority, it nourishes in its bosom a tremendous mass of ignorance, a multitude, a proletariat. Either knowledge must enlarge itself from above or be always in danger of submergence by the ignorant night from below. Still more must it be unsafe if it allows enormous numbers of men to exist outside its pale uninformed by its light, full of the natural vigour of the barbarian, who may at any moment seize upon

## 3. East and West

the physical weapons of the civilised without undergoing an intellectual transformation by their culture. The Graeco-Roman culture perished from within and from without, from without by the floods of Teutonic barbarism, from within by the loss of its vitality."[16]

The effects of this invasion Sri Aurobindo called "the Teutonic lapse". It happened much more gradually than is usually supposed, and many structures of the Roman Empire survived or were revived in due course. Most of these structures or institutions actually belonged to the Catholic Church which before long felt impelled to convert the heathen Teutons. The methods of conversion were far from refined[17], and will have their consequences in the centuries to come, for they resulted in the cruder sides of the Catholic religion and will ultimately lead to the Protestant Reformation. As Sri Aurobindo put it: "The European, ever since the Teutonic mind and temperament took possession of western Europe, has been fundamentally the practical, dynamic and kinetic man, vitalistic in the very marrow of his thought and being. All else has been the fine flower of this

---

16. Sri Aurobindo: *The Human Cycle,* p. 76.
17. The following true anecdote from the time of Louis the Pious (778-840) about the "baptism" of the Danes is an apt illustration. "Each received a white robe from the Emperor's wardrobe, and from his sponsors a full set of Frankish garments, with arms, costly robes and other adornments. This was done repeatedly and more and more [Danes] came each year, not for the sake of Christ but for mundane advantages ... On one occasion as many as fifty arrived. The Emperor asked them if they wished to be baptized. When they had confessed their sins, he ordered them to be sprinkled with holy water. As there were not enough garments to go round on that occasion, Louis ordered some old shirts to be cut up and tacked together to make tunics or to be run up as overalls. When one of these without more ado was put on a certain elderly envoy, he regarded it suspiciously for some time. Then he lost control of himself completely and said to the Emperor: "Look here! I've gone through this ablutions business about twenty times already, and I've always been rigged out before with a splendid white suit; but this old sack makes me feel more like a pig-farmer than a soldier! If it were not for the fact that you've pinched my own clothes and not given me any new ones, with the result that I'd feel a right fool if I walked out of here naked, you could keep your Christ and your reach me downs, too!" (Richard Fletcher: *The Conversion of Europe,* p. 224-25.)

culture, this has been its root and stalk, and in modern times this truth of temperament, always there, has come aggressively to the surface and triumphed over the traditions of Christian piety and Latinistic culture."[18]

"The exceptional nation touched on its higher levels by a developed reason or spirituality or both, as were Greece and later Rome in ancient Europe, India, China and Persia in ancient Asia, is surrounded or neighboured by enormous masses of the old infrarational humanity and endangered by this menacing proximity; for until a developed science comes in to redress the balance, the barbarian has always a greater physical force and unexhausted native power of aggression than the cultured peoples. At this stage the light and power of civilisation always collapses in the end before the attack of the outer darkness. Then ascending Nature has to train the conquerors more or less slowly, with long difficulty and much loss and delay to develop among themselves what their incursion has temporarily destroyed or impaired. *In the end humanity gains by the process; a greater mass of the nations is brought in, a larger and more living force of progress is applied,* a starting-point is reached from which it can move to richer and more varied gains. But a certain loss is always the price of this advance."[19] Readers knowledgeable about the Hegelian view of history will discern in these words of Sri Aurobindo a familiar echo, although Sri Aurobindo's interpretation is much less dogmatic. Hegel sees history as one great curve, one progressively dialectial act of the Spirit; Sri Aurobindo, in his wider view (as we have seen in the first chapter), allows for brilliant progressions as well as dramatic regressions, this being the way in which Nature, the universal Creatrix, encompasses whole peoples and civilisations, thus including them in the upward spiral of the evolution of mankind.

This is how the European Middle Ages came into existence. Their closed universe was geographically based on the western half of the former Roman Empire, which they tried to revive in

---

18. Sri Aurobindo: *The Human Cycle,* p. 157.
19. Id., p. 190 (emphasis added).

one form or another; their world view was a grandiose though rather heterogeneous architecture of a Christianity hardly recognisable from the Gospels, parts of the Roman law and institutions, and fragments of ancient Greek culture; and its basic temper was vitalistic and materialistic, the direct inheritance of the Teutonic tribes. The Catholic Roman Church dominated all forms of life and, passing itself off as the exclusive intermediary, demanded that everybody use its hierarchy to address God. Real spirituality and spiritual experience were mostly foreign to it – and have remained foreign to the West ever since, so much so that Western philosophy and psychology hardly have an inkling of them. But, by reason of the fact that every human being has a soul, spirituality is potentially innate in the human being and in some cases the soul cannot be prevented from coming to the fore, for instance in some saints and mystics. In these cases too a strict conformity with the prescriptions of the Church was a stern demand; nonconformity and a direct approach to the Godhead were branded as heresy, punishable by excommunication and death.

## Humanism and Individualism

The European Middle Ages, with their feudalism, Catholic institutions, crusades, cathedrals, monasteries, universities and scholasticism, was a civilisation that lasted for centuries. Gradually and inevitably, however, the institutions became conventions and the process described by Sri Aurobindo in *The Human Cycle*[20] set in: the conventions were more and more felt as restrictions by sensitive and intelligent people, and a need for individualisation began to be felt. This need formed the basis of the Renaissance and its direct offspring, the Reformation.

"The individualistic age of Europe was in its beginning a revolt of reason, in its culmination a triumphal progress of

---

20. See Chapter 1: "The Big Picture".

physical Science. Such an evolution was historically inevitable. The dawn of individualism is always a questioning, a denial. The individual finds a religion imposed upon him which does not base its dogma and practice upon a living sense of ever verifiable spiritual Truth, but on the letter of an ancient book, the infallible dictum of a Pope, the tradition of a Church, the learned casuistry of schoolmen [the "scholastics"] and Pundits, conclaves of ecclesiastics, heads of monastic orders, doctors of all sorts, all of them unquestionable tribunals whose sole function is to judge and pronounce, but none of whom seems to think it necessary or even allowable to search, test, prove, inquire, discover.

"He [the individual] finds that, as is inevitable under such a regime, true science and knowledge are either banned, punished and persecuted or else rendered obsolete by the habit of blind reliance on fixed authorities; even what is true in old authorities is no longer of any value, because its words are learnedly or ignorantly repeated but its real sense is no longer lived except at most by a few. In politics he finds everywhere divine rights, established privileges, sanctified tyrannies which are evidently armed with an oppressive power and justify themselves by long prescription, but seem to have no real claim or title to exist. In the social order he finds an equally stereotyped reign of convention, fixed disabilities, fixed privileges, the self-regarding arrogance of the high, the blind prostration of the low, while the old functions which might have justified at one time such a distribution of status are either not performed at all or badly performed without any sense of obligation and merely as a part of caste pride.

"He has to rise in revolt; on every claim of authority he has to turn the eye of a resolute inquisition; when he is told that this is the sacred truth of things or the command of God or the immemorial order of human life, he has to reply: 'But is it really so? ... And of all you say, still I must ask, does it agree with the facts of the world, with my sense of right, with my judgment of truth, with my experiences of reality?' And if it does not the revolting individual flings off the yoke, declares the truth as he sees it and in doing so strikes inevitably at the root of the religious, the social, the political, momentarily perhaps even the moral order of the community as it stands, because it stands upon the authority he discredits and the convention he destroys and not upon a living truth which can be successfully opposed to his own. The champions of the old order may be right when they seek to suppress him as a destructive agency perilous to social security, political order or religious tradition; but he stands there and can no other,[21] because to destroy is his mission, to destroy falsehood and lay bare a new foundation of truth."[22]

In these sentences Sri Aurobindo gives the gist of what caused the profound turn in the history of the West (with far-reaching consequences in the global history) that were the Renaissance and the Reformation. Everything the decrepit Catholic Church represented was put into question. But the tenets and the dogmas of the Catholic Church were so ingrained in the Western psyche that even today they keep cropping up in the thinking of writers who deem themselves positivists, materialists, reductionists, atheists. The Reformation was the direct offspring of the Renaissance (its leaders, Luther included, were learned Renaissance men); it was followed by the Enlightenment, the high tide of Reason in the West; the Enlightenment resulted in the American and French Revolutions, followed by the positivist Nineteenth Century, a period of industrialisation, science and progress; and then ensued the "existentialist" Twentieth Century in which the rational systems would lose their bearings and Reason itself, the main tool of disassembly and destruction of the medieval inheritance, would be questioned and even ridiculed.

Why is there this persistent obsession with the Middle Ages? Because they are supposed to have been an Age of Faith in which life had an established and universally accepted meaning,

---

21. This refers to Martin Luther's words before the Diet of Worms, at the critical moment of his revolt against the Pope and the Emperor: "Here I stand, I can no other."
22. Sri Aurobindo: *The Human Cycle*, pp. 16 and 17.

up to a degree justified by rational systems borrowed from the ancient Greeks and from the Arabs. The psychologically defective thought systems of the West never realised – until recently, that is – that Reason is of primary importance but can never be of absolute importance; that the Mind is not a source of knowledge because it cannot really apprehend reality; that the Mind is an essential part of the human being, in the present human condition even its most determinative or characteristic part, but that the human being is far more complex than Cartesian dualism and reductionist materialism have chosen to accept. Since the Middle Ages the West has been desperately in search of a new Faith, mainly through science and (so-called Scientific) Marxism, but both these modern Churches are failing their believers badly. And what to turn to now? This simple question contains in a nutshell the present crisis, which far exceeds the West and has global dimensions.

Europe is taking shape again in the still expanding European Union. One of its numerous problems is a search for identity by its member nations and peoples. What does France represent as such? And Germany? And Great Britain? And Italy? And Poland? And Spain? ... What makes each nation different from the others?[23] And what makes Europe special in the concert of the continents? No doubt the golden thread running through the various phases of Europe's development: humanism and individuality. Recently some philosophers found pleasure in denying the individuality of the human being. (We will touch upon this later.) It may therefore be of importance simply to give a few quotes from Sri Aurobindo on this subject, for his insight is always crystal clear and exactly to the point.

---

23. "The nation or society, like the individual, has a body, an organic life, a moral and aesthetic temperament, a developing mind and a soul behind all these signs and powers for the sake of which they exist. One may see even that, like the individual, it essentially is a soul rather than has one; it is a group-soul that, once having attained to a separate distinctness, must become more and more self-conscious and find itself more and more fully as it develops its corporate action and mentality and its organic self-expressive life." (Sri Aurobindo: *The Human Cycle,* p. 35.)

## 3. East and West

- "The individual is not merely the ephemeral physical creature, a form of mind and body that aggregates and dissolves, but a being, a living power of the eternal Truth, a self-manifesting spirit."[24]

- "The individual is indeed the key of the evolutionary movement; for it is the individual who finds himself, who becomes conscious of the Reality."[25]

- "The immense importance of the individual being, which increases as he rises in the scale, is the most remarkable and significant fact of a universe which started without consciousness and without individuality in an undifferentiated Nescience."[26]

- "The growth of the individual is the indispensable means for the inner growth as distinguished from the outer force and expansion of the collective being. This indeed is the dual importance of the individual that it is through him that the cosmic spirit organises its collective units and makes them self-expressive and progressive and through him that it raises Nature from the Inconscience to the Superconscience and exalts it to meet the Transcendent."[27]

- "It is always the individual who receives the intuitions of Nature and takes the step forward dragging or drawing the rest of humanity behind him ... For a mass experience or discovery or expression is not the first method of Nature; it is at some one point or a few points that the fire is lit and spreads from hearth to hearth, from altar to altar."[28]

- *"The principle of individualism is the liberty of the human being regarded as a separate existence to develop himself and fulfil his life, satisfy his mental tendencies, emotional and vital needs and physical being according to his own desire governed by his reason;*

---

24. Sri Aurobindo: *The Human Cycle,* p. 35.
25. Sri Aurobindo: *The Life Divine,* p. 1050.
26. Id., p. 755.
27. Id., pp. 692-93.
28. Id., pp. 869-80.

*it admits no other limit to this right and this liberty except the obligation to respect the same individual liberty and right in others.*"[29]

- "The great evolutionary periods of humanity have taken place in communities where the individual became active, mentally, vitally or spiritually alive. For this reason Nature invented the ego that the individual might disengage himself from the inconscience or subconscience of the mass and become an independent living mind, life-power, soul, spirit, co-ordinating himself with the world around him but not drowned in it and separately inexistent and ineffective. For the individual is indeed part of the cosmic being, but he is also something more, he is a soul that has descended from the Transcendence. This he cannot manifest at once, because he is too near to the cosmic Inconscience, not near enough to the original Superconscience; he has to find himself as the mental and vital ego before he can find himself as the soul or spirit."[30]

- "Whatever perfection of the collectivity is to be sought after, can come only by the perfection of the individuals who constitute it."[31]

- "But within this general nature and general destiny of mankind each individual human being has to follow the common aim on the lines of his own nature and to arrive at his possible perfection by a growth from within ... He is not merely the noble, merchant, warrior, priest, scholar, artist, cultivator or artisan, not merely the religionist or the worldling or the politician. Nor can he be limited by his nationality; he is not merely the Englishman or the Frenchman, the Japanese or the Indian; if by a part of himself he belongs to the nation, by another he exceeds it and belongs to humanity. And even there is a part of him, the greatest, which is not limited by humanity; he belongs by it to God

---

29. Sri Aurobindo: *The Human Cycle*, p. 55 (emphasis added).
30. Sri Aurobindo: *The Life Divine*, p. 694.
31. Id., p. 696.

## 3. East and West

and to the world of all beings and to the godheads of the future."[32]

- "But in addition there is this deeper truth which individualism has discovered, that the individual is not merely a social unit; his existence, his right and claim to live and grow are not founded solely on his social work and function. He is not merely a member of a human pack, hive or ant-hill; he is something in himself, a soul, a being, who has to fulfil his own individual truth and law as well as his natural or his assigned part in the truth and law of the collective existence. He demands freedom, space, initiative for his soul, for his nature, for that puissant and tremendous thing which society so much distrusts and has laboured in the past either to suppress altogether or to relegate to the purely spiritual field, an individual thought, will and conscience. If he is to merge these eventually, it cannot be into the dominating thought, will and conscience of others, but into something beyond into which he and all must be both allowed and helped freely to grow. That is an idea, a truth which, intellectually recognised and given its full exterior and superficial significance by Europe, agrees at its root with the profoundest and highest spiritual conceptions of Asia and has a large part to play in the moulding of the future."[33]

- "It is in Europe that the age of individualism has taken birth and exercised its full sway; the East has entered it only by contact and influence, not from an original impulse. And it is to its passion for the discovery of the actual truth of things and for the governing of human life by whatever law of the truth it has found that the West owes its centuries of strength, vigour, light, progress, irresistible expansion."[34]

The individualisation of the human being, rooted in the Earth that is its Mother and yet availing of the possibility to be

---

32. Sri Aurobindo: *The Human Cycle*, p. 69.
33. Id., p. 24.
34. Id., pp. 15 and 16.

completely in possession of itself, is without any doubt the great realisation of Europe. The men and women of the present day are hardly aware of the debt they owe to so many daring and tireless thinkers, dreamers and seers of the past for the freedom to be themselves in ways unprecedented in history. Countless are the individuals in Greece, among the first Christians, during the Renaissance, Reformation, Enlightenment and the two great revolutions to which it led, who dedicated and even sacrificed their lives to this freedom of self-mastery. Never has individualism been more widespread than now – more used and, what still is inevitable among humans, abused.

Today in most parts of the world man and woman can be themselves. Ultimately they are accountable only to themselves. Many are frightened by this responsibility. It is, however, the only way to see oneself whole, to experience oneself fully, and, in the last instance, to discover one's real self within. There awaits the Light; there is the unshakeable foundation; there is hidden the secret that is the key – the only one – to ourselves, the universe, and the meaning of it all. Deep inside is present the true Individual who supports the surface individual before its birth, during its life, after its death.

The work and suffering of centuries, the true treasure gathered by Europe, will prove its value; it will lead the descendants of the Teutons and the descendants of all the tribes they have mixed with to something that until now remained outside their ken: the spiritual experience – the direct, personal, individual encounter with God.

## The Eastern Way – India

To find what the West is lacking, the spiritual experience, we have to turn to the East, more especially to India, "the heart of Asia", whose spiritual attainments have spread across the whole of Eastern Asia in the form of Buddhism, in South-East

## 3. East and West

Asia in the form of Brahmanism, and in West Asia through its influence on Christianity.

Few have had such a high, and well-founded, opinion of India as Sri Aurobindo and the Mother. Here are some of their statements by way of illustration. "In the whole of creation the earth has a place of distinction, because unlike any other planet it is evolutionary with a psychic entity at its centre", wrote the Mother. "In it, India, in particular, is a divinely chosen country." – "India is not the earth, rivers and mountains of this land, neither is it a collective name for the inhabitants of this country. India is a living being, as much living as, say, Shiva. India is a goddess as Shiva is a god. If she likes, she can manifest in human form." – "India has become the symbolic representation of all the difficulties of modern mankind. India will be the land of its resurrection – the resurrection to a higher and true life." – "It is only India's soul who can unify the country." – "India is the country where the psychic law can and must rule and the time has come for that here." – "It is only to those who can conquer the mind's preferences and prejudices of race and education that India reveals the mystery of her treasure."[35]

"We have a flag which Sri Aurobindo called the Spiritual Flag of United India", wrote the Mother, who designed it. "Its square form, its colour and every detail of its design have a symbolic meaning. It was hoisted on the 15th August 1947 when India became free. It will now be hoisted on the 1st November 1954 when these settlements [the French enclaves on the subcontinent] get united with India and it will be hoisted in the future whenever India recovers other parts of herself. United India has a special mission to fulfil in the world. Sri Aurobindo laid down his life for it and we are prepared to do the same."[36] The Mother also drew a map of the real India, the still divided physical embodiment of India's soul. "The map was made after the partition [in 1947]. It is the map of the true India, in spite of all passing appearances, and it will always remain the map of

---
35. *Words of the Mother*, CWM 13, pp. 376, 380, 376 (2x), 378 (emphasis in the text) and 382.
36. Id., p. 362.

the true India, whatever people may think of it."[37] It includes the present India, Pakistan, Sikkim, Bhutan, Bangladesh, part of Burma and Sri Lanka.[38]

Sri Aurobindo and the Mother's extreme stand on India was not the result of irrational patriotic fervour and certainly not a pose. Several selections of their positive statements about India have been published, but usually without mentioning their comments on the past and present negative aspects of India's development. "Certainly we must repel with vigour every disintegrating or injurious attack [on India and its culture]", wrote Sri Aurobindo, "but it is much more important to form our own true and independent view of our own past achievement, present position and future possibilities, – what we were, what we are and what we may be. In our past we must distinguish all that was great, essential, elevating, vitalising, illuminating, victorious, effective. And in that again we must distinguish what was close to the permanent, essential spirit and the persistent law of our cultural being and separate from it what was temporary and transiently formulative. *For all that was great in the past cannot be preserved as it was or repeated forever; there are new needs, there are other vistas before us.* But we have to distinguish too what was deficient, ill-grasped, imperfectly formulated or only suited to the limiting needs of the age or unfavourable circumstances.

"For it is quite idle to pretend that all in the past, even at

---

37. Id., p. 368.
38. In the text of a radio message to be delivered on 15 August 1947, Sri Aurobindo wrote: "The old communal division into Hindu and Muslim seems to have hardened into the figure of a permanent political division of the country. It is to be hoped that the Congress and the nation will not accept the settled fact as forever settled or as anything more than a temporary expedient. For if it lasts, India may be seriously weakened, even crippled: civil strife may remain always possible, possible even a new invasion and foreign conquest. The partition of the country must go ... By whatever means, the division must and will go. For without it the destiny of India might be seriously impaired and even frustrated. But that must not be." (Sri Aurobindo: *On Himself,* p. 402. It is worth recalling here that Sri Aurobindo had been one of the prominent freedom fighters of his country, the very first to demand its unconditional and total independence.)

its greatest, was entirely admirable and in its kind the highest consummate achievement of the human mind and spirit. Afterwards we have to make a comparison of this past with our present and to understand the causes of our decline and seek the remedy of our shortcomings and ailments. Our sense of the greatness of our past must not be made a fatally hypnotising lure to inertia; it should be rather an inspiration to renewed and greater achievement. But in our criticism of the present we must not be one-sided or condemn with a foolish impartiality all that we are or have done. Neither flattering or glossing over our downfall nor fouling our nest to win the applause of the stranger, we have to note our actual weakness and its roots, but to fix too our eyes with a still firmer attention on our elements of strength, our abiding potentialities, our dynamic impulses of self-renewal."[39] The importance of these masterfully formulated words is perhaps greater at present than at the time they were written.

It is now generally forgotten that India once was an opulent civilisation and the wonder of the world. The cause of its impoverishment and deterioration was, according to Sri Aurobindo and the Mother, the otherworldly mentality propagated by Buddhism and illusionism. "In India the philosophy of world-negation has been given formulations of supreme power and value by two of the greatest of her thinkers, Buddha and Shankara ... The spirit of these two remarkable spiritual philosophies, – for Shankara in the historical process of India's philosophical mind takes up, completes and replaces Buddha, – has weighed with a tremendous power on the thought, religion and general mentality: everywhere broods its mighty shadow, everywhere is the impress of the three great formulas, the chain of *Karma,* escape from the wheel of rebirth, Maya."[40] – "Buddha and Shankara supposed the world to be radically false and miserable; therefore escape from the world was to them the only wisdom. But this world is Brahman, the world is God, the world is *Satyam*

---

39. Sri Aurobindo: The *Renaissance in India*, pp. 87-88 (emphasis added).
40. Sri Aurobindo: *The Life Divine,* pp. 415-16.

[Truth], the world is Ananda [Bliss]; it is our misreading of the world through mental egoism that is a falsehood and our wrong relation with God in the world that is misery. There is no other falsity and no other cause of sorrow."[41]

"We have then to return to the pursuit of an ancient secret which man, as a race, has seen only obscurely and followed after lamely, has indeed understood only with his surface mind and not in its heart of meaning, – and yet in following it lies his social no less than his individual salvation, – the ideal of the Kingdom of God, the secret of the reign of the Spirit over mind and life and body. It is because they have never quite lost hold of this secret, never disowned it in impatience for a lesser victory, that the older Asiatic nations have survived so persistently and can now, as if immortal, raise their faces towards a new dawn; for they have fallen asleep [this was written during the First World War], but they have not perished. It is true that they have for a time failed in life, where the European nations who trusted to the flesh and the intellect have succeeded; but that success, speciously complete but only for a time, has always turned into a catastrophe. Still Asia had failed in life, she had fallen in the dust, and even if the dust in which she was lying was sacred, as the modern poet of Asia [Rabindranath Tagore] has declared, – though the sacredness may be doubted, – still the dust is not the proper place for man, nor is to lie prostrate in it his right human attitude."[42]

"The need of a developing humanity is not to return always to its old ideas. Its need is to progress to a larger fulfilment in which, if the old is at all taken up, it must be transformed and exceeded. For the underlying truth of things is constant and eternal, but its mental figures, its life forms, its physical embodiment call constantly for growth and change.

"In India, since the great Buddhistic upheaval of the national thought and life, there has been a series of recurrent attempts to rediscover the truth of the soul and life and get behind the

---

41. Sri Aurobindo: *Essays Divine and Human*, p. 96.
42. Sri Aurobindo: *The Human Cycle*, pp. 239-40.

## 3. East and West

veil of stifling conventions; but these have been conducted by a wide and tolerant spiritual reason, a plastic soul-intuition and deep subjective seeking, insufficiently militant and destructive. Although productive of great internal and considerable external changes, they have never succeeded in getting rid of the predominant conventional order ...

"It is only with the period of European influence and impact that circumstances and tendencies powerful enough to enforce the beginnings of a new age of radical and effective revaluation of ideas and things have come into existence. The characteristic power of these influences has been throughout – or at any rate till quite recently – rationalistic, utilitarian and individualistic. It has compelled the national mind to view everything from a new, searching and critical standpoint, and even those who seek to preserve the present or restore the past are obliged unconsciously or half-consciously to justify their endeavour from the novel point of view and by its appropriate standards of reasoning. Throughout the East, the subjective Asiatic mind is being driven to adapt itself to the need for changed values of life and thought. It has been forced to turn upon itself both by the pressure of western knowledge and by the compulsion of a quite changed life-need and life-environment. What it did not do from within, has come on it as a necessity from without and this externality has carried with it an immense advantage as well as great dangers."[43]

In these paragraphs Sri Aurobindo has summarised clearly the ancient secret, guarded in "the heart of an Asia" that fell asleep with it and that was awakened by European colonialism in search of material riches and dominion. It may, however, turn out that the ultimate boon of the colonialists' efforts will be something they could have no idea of: that India will share its spiritual treasure with the West. What kind of treasure is this?

"The East is on the whole, in spite of certain questionings and scruples, willing and, where not wholly willing, forced by

---

43. Id., p. 17.

circumstances and the general tendency of mankind to accept the really valuable parts of modern European culture, its science, its curiosity, its ideal of universal education and uplift, its abolition of privilege, its instinct of freedom and equality, its call for the breaking down of narrow and oppressive forms, for air, space, light. But at a certain point the East refuses to proceed farther and that is precisely in the things which are deepest, most essential to the future of mankind. The things of the soul, the profound things of the mind and temperament. Here, again, all points not to substitution and conquest, but to mutual understanding and interchange, mutual adaptation and new formation."[44]

## The Spiritual Experience

Then what is that essential element, spirituality, which is unknown to the West? "Spirituality is not a high intellectuality, not idealism, not an ethical turn of mind or moral purity and austerity, not religiosity or an ardent and exalted emotional fervour, not even a compound of all these excellent things", writes Sri Aurobindo in *The Life Divine;* "a mental belief, creed or faith, an emotional aspiration, a regulation of conduct according to a religious or ethical formula are not spiritual achievement and experience. These things are of considerable value to mind and life; they are of value to the spiritual evolution itself as preparatory movements disciplining, purifying or giving a suitable form to the nature; but they still belong to the mental evolution, – the beginning of a spiritual realisation, experience, change is not yet there. *Spirituality is in its essence an awakening of the inner reality of our being, to a spirit, self, soul which is other than our mind, life and body, an inner aspiration to know, to feel to be that, to enter into contact with the greater Reality beyond and pervading the universe which inhabits also our own being, to be in communion with*

---

44. Id., p. 321.

*It and union with It, and a turning, a conversion, a transformation of our whole being as a result of the aspiration, the contact, the union, a growth or waking into a new becoming or new being, a new self, a new nature.*"[45] All Christians will assert that they have a soul, but few will be able to say what it is, except that it is in some way immortal. The soul, the real individual and, according to Sri Aurobindo in the aforementioned paragraph, the key to all things spiritual, is the essence and ground of our being; it is the divine spark in us which grows as the psychic being in whatever may be our spiritual destiny. It is the presence of the Divine in his manifestation. Because of our soul we are not only the Sons and Daughters of Man but also the Sons and Daughters of God. Read the Western philosophers, worldly or religious, and you will find the soul confounded or identified with the vital being, with the mind, or with both, so widespread is the confusion concerning what we should understand with utter clarity because it is the mainspring of our life, the lever of our becoming, and that what we were, are and will be in eternity – the golden Light within, our glory and ecstasy of being.

The second means of acquiring spiritual knowledge and experience is by gaining access to the spiritual levels above the mind: higher mind, illumined mind, intuition and overmind.[46] "In the East, especially in India, the metaphysical thinkers have tried, as in the West, to determine the nature of the highest Truth by the intellect. They have, however, not given mental thinking the supreme rank as an instrument in the discovery of Truth, but only a secondary status. The first rank has always been given to spiritual intuition and illumination and spiritual experience; an intellectual conclusion that contradicts this supreme authority is held invalid ... Each philosophical founder (as also those who continued his work or school) has been a metaphysical thinker doubled with a yogi. Those who were only philosophic intellectuals were respected for their learning but never took rank as truth-discoverers."[47]

---

45. Sri Aurobindo: *The Life Divine*, p. 857 (emphasis added).
46. See Chapter 4 in *Overman* by Georges Van Vrekhem.
47. Sri Aurobindo: *Letters on Yoga*, p. 159.

"The sages of the Veda and Vedanta relied entirely upon intuition and spiritual experience. It is by an error that scholars sometimes speak of great debates or discussions in the Upanishad. Wherever there is the appearance of a controversy, it is not by discussion, by dialectics or the use of logical reasoning that it proceeds, but by a comparison of intuitions and experiences in which the less luminous gives place to the more luminous, the narrower, faultier or less essential to the more comprehensive, more perfect, more essential. The question asked by one sage of another is 'What dost thou know?', not 'What dost thou think?' nor 'To what conclusion has thy reasoning arrived?' Nowhere in the Upanishads do we find any trace of logical reasoning urged in support of the truths of Vedanta. Intuition, the sages seem to have held, must be corrected by a more perfect intuition; logical reasoning cannot be its judge."[48]

By way of comment. Firstly, "intuition" here is not what is meant by this word in the common parlance: a hint, a feeling, a presentiment, a suspicion, or whatever to the same effect. By "intuition" Sri Aurobindo and the Mother mean a "knowledge by identity", which is the only real knowledge; it is proper to the spiritual level of the same name; it is "a messenger from the superconscient and therefore our highest faculty". – "Intuition always stands veiled behind our mental operations. Intuition brings to man those brilliant messages from the Unknown which are the beginning of his higher knowledge. Reason only comes afterwards to see what profit it can have of the shining harvest. Intuition gives us that idea of something behind and beyond all that we know and seem to be which pursues man always in contradiction of his lower reason and all his normal experience and impels him to formulate that formless perception in the more positive ideas of God, Immortality, Heaven and the rest by which we strive to express it to the mind ... Ancient Vedanta seized this message of the Intuition and formulated it in the three great declarations of the *Upanishads*, 'I am He', 'Thou art

---

48. Sri Aurobindo: *The Life Divine*, p. 69.

That, O Swetaketu', 'All this is the Brahman, this Self is the Brahman.'"[49]

Secondly, ancient India had a broader gamut of philosophical schools, including even purely materialist ones, than the West has had since Descartes. The true foundation of rational thinking, however, remained always the spiritual levels beyond the rational mind. The image of the human being in the West is still distressingly limited and defective; its limitation perforce afflicts its philosophical reasoning and causes its inability to solve any fundamental problem. As we will see in the next chapter, this has led in the present time to a fallow ground of philosophical absurdity where anything goes and nothing is real or true anymore. "One must transgress limits and penetrate to the knowledge behind, which must be experienced before it can be known; for the ear hears it, the intellect observes it, but the spirit alone can possess it. Realisation in the self of things is the only knowledge; all else is mere idea or opinion,"[50] wrote Sri Aurobindo. And, ever the radical: "It is irrelevant to me what Max Müller thinks of the Veda or what Sayana thinks of the Veda. I should prefer to know what the Veda has to say for itself and, if there is any light there on the unknown or on the infinite, to follow the ray till I come face to face with that which it illumines."[51]

"I seek a text and a Shastra", Sri Aurobindo wrote, "that is not subject to interpolation, modification and replacement, that moth and white ant cannot destroy, that the earth cannot bury nor Time mutilate ... I believe that Veda [i.e. Knowledge] to be the foundation of the *Sanatana Dharma*; I believe it to be the concealed divinity within Hinduism, – but a veil has to be drawn aside, a curtain has to be lifted. I believe it to be knowable and discoverable. I believe the future of India and the world to depend on its discovery and on its application, not to the renunciation of life, but to life in the world and among men."[52] – "You

---

49. Id., pp. 68-67.
50. Sri Aurobindo: *Essays Divine and Human*, p. 34.
51. Id., p. 35.
52. Id., p. 62.

will find disputants questioning your system on the ground that it is not consistent with this or that *Shastra* [Scripture] or this or that great authority, whether philosopher, saint or Avatar. *Remember then that realisation and experience are alone of essential importance.* What Shankara argued or Vivekananda conceived intellectually about existence or even what Ramakrishna stated from his multitudinous and varied realisation, is only of value to you so far as you [are] moved by God to accept and renew it in your own experience. The opinions of thinkers and saints and Avatars should be accepted as hints but not as fetters. What matters to you is what you have seen or what God in his universal personality or impersonality or again personally in some teacher, guru or pathfinder undertakes to show you in the path of Yoga."[53]

## Conclusion

> *The West is reawakening to the truth of the spirit and the spiritual possibilities of life, the East is reawakening to the truth of Life and tends towards a new application to it of its spiritual knowledge.*[54]
>
> – Sri Aurobindo

It is evident, at this decisive turn in the history of humanity, that the West desperately seeks to fill up the emptiness of its inner life since the erosion of the certainties of the medieval faith, and that therefore it is more and more turning towards the treasures of spirituality preserved in the East, more particularly in India. The West has worked hard to make the existence of the individual human being, man and woman, possible; this is a necessary and essential achievement in the development of humanity. Man and woman are now, for the first time in history

---
53. Id., p. 105 (emphasis added).
54. Sri Aurobindo: *Essays in Philosophy and Yoga*, p. 106.

## 3. East and West

on a general scale, at last directly responsible for themselves but also confronted with themselves, with what they really are in their essence, with their selves. The nature of the self is a knowledge kept alive in the East, and so are the techniques for its discovery and the ways of living in it.

The mental climate of the West is still very distrustful of Eastern wisdom. For centuries the West has been convinced of its superiority, intellectually and religiously. The founder of its faith was the only Avatar, Jesus Christ, the one and only incarnation of God as man, of the Son of God who was also the Son of Man; the Christian institutions based on this faith were the only ones to possess the means of the salvation and the keys of heaven. Everything outside these institutions was condemned as primitivism and idolatry, as darkness peopled by demons. And when the Western faith became anaemic, when its image of God faded, science replaced it with a worldview no less dogmatic than the creed of the Churches. These factors created an almost instinctive suspicion, not to say aversion, of anything Eastern – except in the soul of more and more individuals who instinctively, if not rationally, felt that the Eastern spiritual paths were worth exploring, that following them one could breathe and be oneself in freedom, that they provided the possibility to meet directly with God and at last justify life on Earth.

To a Western world still imprisoned within its prejudices, Sri Aurobindo addressed the following words: "To refuse to enquire upon any general ground preconceived and a priori is an obscurantism as prejudicial to the extension of knowledge as the religious obscurantism which opposed in Europe the extension of scientific discovery. The greatest inner discoveries, the experience of self-being, the cosmic consciousness, the inner calm of the liberated spirit, the direct effect of mind upon mind, the knowledge of things by consciousness in direct contact with other consciousness or with its objects, most spiritual experiences of any value, cannot be brought before the tribunal of the common mentality which has no experience of these things and takes its own absence or incapacity of experience as a proof of their incapacity or their non-existence. Physical truth of formulas, generalisations, discoveries founded upon physical observation can be so referred, but even there a training of capacity is needed before one can truly understand and judge; it is not every untrained mind that can follow the mathematics of relativity or other difficult scientific truths or judge of the validity either of their result or their process.

"All reality, all experience must indeed, to be held as true, be capable of verification by a same or similar experience; so, in fact, all men can have a spiritual experience and can follow it out and verify it in themselves, but only when they have acquired the capacity or can follow the inner methods by which that experience and verification are made possible. It is necessary to dwell for a moment on these obvious and elementary truths because the opposite ideas have been sovereign in a recent period of human mentality, – they are now only receding, – and have stood in the way of the development of a vast domain of possible knowledge. It is of supreme importance for the human spirit to be free to sound the depths of inner or subliminal reality, of spiritual and of what is still superconscient reality, and not to immure itself in the physical mind and its narrow domain of objective external solidities; for in that way alone can there come liberation from the Ignorance in which our mentality dwells and a release into a complete consciousness, a true and integral self-realisation and self-knowledge."[55]

The following is an extract from Sri Aurobindo's "Message to America", given on 15 August 1949. "It has been customary to dwell on the division and difference between these two sections of the human family [East and West] and even to oppose them to each other; but for myself I would rather be disposed to dwell on oneness and unity than on division and difference. East and West have the same human nature, a common human destiny, the same aspiration after a greater perfection, the same seeking after something higher than itself, something towards which inwardly and even outwardly we move. There has been a tendency in some minds to dwell on the spirituality or mysticism

---

55. Sri Aurobindo: *The Life Divine,* pp. 650-51.

of the East and the materialism of the West; but the West has had no less than the East its spiritual seekings and, though not in such profusion, its saints and sages and mystics, the East has had its materialistic tendencies, its material splendours, its similar or identical dealings with life and Matter and the world in which we live. East and West have always met and mixed more or less closely, they have powerfully influenced each other and at the present day are under an increasing compulsion of Nature and Fate to do so more than ever before.

"There is a common hope, a common destiny, both spiritual and material, for which both are needed as coworkers. It is no longer towards division and difference that we should turn our minds but on unity, union, even oneness necessary for the pursuit and realisation of a common ideal, the destined goal, the fulfilment towards which Nature in her beginning obscurely set out and must in an increasing light of knowledge replacing her first ignorance constantly persevere."[56]

Sri Aurobindo was asked for a message to be broadcast by the Trichinopoly station of All India Radio on 15 August 1947, the day of India's independence. In this message he enumerated the world movements which once had "looked like impossible dream" of his, but which were "on this day either approaching fruition" or "on the way to their achievement". The fourth of these dreams – we will encounter them in a subsequent chapter – was "the gift by India of her spiritual knowledge and her means for the spiritualisation of life to the whole race": "The spiritual gift of India to the world has already begun. India's spirituality is entering Europe and America in an ever-increasing measure. That movement will grow; amid the disasters of the time more and more eyes are turning towards her with hope and there is even an increasing resort not only to her teachings, but to her psychic and spiritual practice."[57]

The materialisation of Sri Aurobindo's prediction on the threshold of the new millennium is there for all to see. As

---

56. Sri Aurobindo: *On Himself*, p. 414.
57. Id., pp. 401 ff.

Roger-Pol Droit writes in his remarkable book *L'Oubli de l'Inde* (Forgetting India): by the joining of the most precious values of East and West, it will at last be possible for "the complete man" to be born. "From Herodotus to Montaigne, [man, according to the Western view] only inhabited the shores of the Mediterranean ... [His destiny] took shape between the delta of the Nile, the land of Judea and the coasts of Greece. Or between Byzantium, Rome and the Rhine. Never beyond the Elbrus or in the plains of the Ganges. Now the discovery of Asia will make possible the unification of the two halves of the world. It will allow to foresee the espousal of humanity with itself and the advent of a new humanist thinking, richer and at the same time much more supple."[58] If Sri Aurobindo and the Mother are correct, it may well be that what is awaiting humanity is far beyond a new, more complete form of humanist thinking: from humanity will first emerge an overhuman, and afterwards a supramental, divine species.

---

58. Roger-Pol Droit: *L'Oubli de l'Inde,* pp. 116-17.

# 4
Reason on Trial

*The Age of Reason is visibly drawing to an end.*[1]

– Sri Aurobindo

*Why, in fact, are we attached to the truth? Why the truth rather than lies? Why the truth rather than myth? Why the truth rather than illusion?*[2]

– Michel Foucault

"The history of the twenty years after 1973 is that of a world which lost its bearings and slid into instability and crisis,"[3] writes Eric Hobsbawm, one of the few genuinely great historians of our century. He is not the only intellectual who entered the gates of the Third Millennium in a state of befuddlement; actually, there were and are a few others. Humanity seems to have lost its bearings as early as in "the tumult of the 1960s", or rather it has lost its head, its reason, its mental capacities of rationalisation, understanding, and concentration.

The mental chaos was to be expected if the view of Sri Aurobindo and the Mother, and the forces activated by their Work, contain any truth. Man is "the mental being" par excellence, as one finds repeated time and again in their books. If man has to be surpassed by the overman and afterwards by the supramental being, then reason, the mental being's main means of consciousness, must be surpassed – something painfully traumatic and profoundly puzzling to a being that relies on reason as its principal means of awareness and expression, and that

---
1. Sri Aurobindo: *The Human Cycle*, p. 23.
2. In: *The Fontana Post-Modern Reader*, p. 41.
3. Eric Hobsbawm: *The Age of Extremes*, p. 403.

even deems reason to be the highest phenomenon achieved by evolution. How can the highest be surpassed except by what to the mind seems sheer irrationality, chaos, or nothingness? A transitional period with the eventual aim of the transformation of mankind must of necessity put all certainties into question and do away with most of them to make place for new ones that cannot be imagined. This period of transition the Mother once called, only partly in jest, "the supramental catastrophe". Humanity, and through it the world, is undergoing a sea change. That reason lost its moorings is one of the consequences, only explainable from the Aurobindonian perspective.

## Postmodernism

Culturally speaking, the period that begun in the 1960s and that is still continuing, is known as "postmodernism". This rather awkward buzzword, "a makeshift word", actually says nothing about the period we are in as it refers to the previous period, the last of the past. "Postmodernism" is applicable to the present philosophical trend as well as to science, industrialism, art, architecture, literature, and fashion. It evokes something multifaceted, varied, undetermined, unbounded, heterogeneous, chaotic, disordered, improvised, confused, vibrant, colourful, grotesque and even nihilistic. A few definitions by experts may give the reader an idea of the indefinable because not yet overseeable and therefore not apprehendable.

- "We must reconcile ourselves to a paradoxical-sounding thought: namely, the thought that we no longer live in the 'modern' world. The 'modern' world is now a thing of the past. Our own natural science today is no longer 'modern' science. Instead ... it is rapidly engaged in becoming 'postmodern' science: the science to the 'postmodern' world, of 'postnationalist' politics and 'postindustrial' society – the

## 4. Reason on Trial

world that has not yet discovered how to define itself in terms of what is, but only in terms of what it has just-now ceased to be."[4] (Stephen Toulmin)

- "Although many at first dismissed the postmodern turn as a fad and have been predicting its demise for years, postmodern discourses continue to proliferate and attract interest, winning fervent advocates and passionate opponents. The term 'postmodern' is thus increasingly taken as a synonym for the contemporary social moment and as a marker to describe its novelties and its differences from modern culture and society. Yet there is no agreement on what constitutes the postmodern, on whether we are indeed in a new postmodern era, or on what theories best illuminate the dynamics and experiences of the contemporary moment."[5] (Stephen Best and Douglas Kellner)

- "Philosophical opinion regarding the postmodern family [the various disciplines to which the word is applied] is deeply divided. For some, postmodernism connotes the final escape from the stultifying legacy of modern European theology, metaphysics, authoritarianism, colonialism, racism, and domination. To others it represents the attempt by disgruntled left-wing intellectuals to destroy Western civilisation. To yet others it labels a goofy collection of hermetically obscure writers who are really talking about nothing at all ...

- "When most philosophers use the word 'postmodernism' they mean to refer to a movement that developed in France in the 1960s ... along with subsequent and related developments. They have in mind that this movement denies the possibility of objective knowledge of the real world, 'univocal' (single or primary) meaning of words and texts, the unity of the human self, the cogency of the distinctions between rational inquiry and political action, literal and

---
4. In *The Fontana Post-Modern Reader*, p. 3.
5. Stephen Best and Douglas Kellner: *The Postmodern Turn*, p. ix.

metaphorical meaning, science and art, and even the possibility of truth itself."[6] (Lawrence Cahoone).

- "Postmodern discourse articulates *fin-de-siècle* anxieties concerning the end of an era and the demise of certainties, orthodoxies, and positions that have sustained thought and politics over the past three centuries. Shedding of old habits of thought and action is often difficult; thus the postmodern turn evokes threats and challenges that are often anxiety producing, although, as noted, it also contains exciting challenges and experiences. It is curious that apocalyptic thought frequently erupts at the close of a century, and as the 20th century comes to an end there are many who see an entire world order – modernity – dissolving as an uncertain future quickly approaches (or is already here)."[7] (Stephen Best and Douglas Kellner)

- "Postmodernism is often associated with a revolt against order, representation, narrative, system and signification, and a tendency towards eclecticism, irony, parody, quotation, self-referentiality and indeterminacy ... [Its philosophical framework is that of] late-20th-century philosophies of demystification, decanonisation and decentring which move beyond humanist notions of subject and object, nature and being and the 'modern' project of the Enlightenment ...

- "Indeed, according to Charles Jencks, 'In the last ten years post-modernism has become more than a social condition and cultural movement, it has become a world view.' Recent studies have emphasized this, devoting themselves not simply to artistic and cultural phenomena but to the changing paradigm of the age ... Frederic Jameson has it that 'postmodernism is what you have when the modernization process is complete and nature is gone for good', creating a world of simulacra, commodity fetishism, narcissism, affectless eroticism, depthless history, and, in cultural

---

6. Lawrence Cahoone (ed.): *From Modernism to Postmodernism*, pp. 1 and 2.
7. Stephen Best and Douglas Kellner: op. cit. p. 15.

## 4. Reason on Trial

expression, 'the first specifically North American global style'."[8] (Malcolm Bradbury)

This might be summarised as follows: the contemporary period in history, provisionally labelled "postmodern", turns against the "modern" period – Reformation, Enlightenment and 19th century – by which it was engendered, but whose "stultifying legacy" of values proves to be unreliable, misleading and even false; the "certainties" transmitted by the "modern" to the present world turn out to be no longer applicable; postmodern man and woman, therefore, do not possess the intellectual standards to interpret and understand the overwhelming newness of the world that is theirs.

The fundamental problem, however, is that the "modern" period represented "the triumph of reason" and that as the postmoderns found out, *reason, i.e. the rational mind, is unable to produce truth and even to comprehend it*. The modern period has been unable to provide a ground of truth on which to build one's personality, one's society and one's outlook on the future. As pointed out in the preceding chapter, the whole of the modern period can be seen as a reaction of the human reason against the "unreasonable", irrational period of faith we call the Middle Ages. In the Middle Ages there was a generally accepted system of belief concerning the conception of man, of the world, and of God. This system, the world view of Catholic Christianity in Western Europe, had elementary limitations and flaws which one day would have to be brought to the surface if *homo europaeus* was to fulfil his destiny, his part in the evolution of humankind. The criticism of the medieval world view started with the reactivation of the rational mind of ancient Greece; its rediscovery created the Renaissance. The 18th century Enlightenment is also called the Age of Reason. The 19th century philosophical and sociological thinkers prided themselves on having cleared the human mind of all remnants

---

8. In: *The New Fontana Dictionary of Modern Thought*, pp. 674-75 passim.

of irrationality (Comte's positivism and Marxism were supposed to be "scientific"). The 20th century proved all of them to be badly mistaken.

That the postmodern kaleidoscopic bedlam is caused by a misvaluation of reason is apparent from the following. Among the themes of postmodernity are, according to Steinar Kvale "a doubt that any human truth is a simple objective representation of reality", "a focus on the way societies use language to construct their own realities", and "a belief that reason appears in many guises."[9] In other words, reason cannot discover or formulate truth; there is no (general) truth as such, and if there is it cannot be known. "All meanings and truths are never absolute or timeless, but are always framed by socially and historically specific conditions of knowledge."[10]

"Seeing truth as made, not found – seeing reality as socially constructed – doesn't mean deciding there is nothing 'out there'. It means understanding that all our stories about what's out there – all our scientific facts, our religious teachings, our society's beliefs, even our personal perceptions – are the products of a highly creative interaction between human minds and the cosmos. The cosmos may be found; but the ideas we form about it, and the things we say about it, are made. One of the main themes of postmodern thought is that language is deeply involved in the social construction of reality. [The American philosopher Richard] Rorty says: 'We need to make a distinction between the claim that the world is out there and the claim that truth is out there. To say that the world is out there, that it is not our creation, is to say, with common sense, that most things in space and time are the effects of causes that do not include human mental states. To say that truth is not out there is simply to say that where there are no sentences there is no truth, that sentences are elements of human languages, and that human languages are human creations.'"[11] (Walter T. Anderson)

Conclusion: postmodernism says that truth is a human

---
9. *The Fontana Reader of Postmodernism*, p. 18.
10. Glenn Ward: *Postmodernism*, p. 96.
11. *The Fontana Postmodern Reader*, p. 8.

## 4. Reason on Trial

creation, as varied (and partial) as the humans who create it, be they individuals or societies. Consequences: according to postmodernism 1. There is no such thing as a "true self", the individual does not exist on a ground of being;"[12] 2. There are no "grand narratives" (metanarratives, *métarécits*), i.e. true philosophical systems, world views, religions. All is relative, a changing part of changing wholes, structures, complex (and accidental) "events". Small wonder that this way of seeing things easily turns into nihilism on the one hand and extreme subjectivism, now sometimes called "narcissism", on the other.

This may be shocking to people who believe in essences and in an objective, experienceable truth; yet, it is not amazing considering the philosophical and historical elements of the life and thought of Western man. For wasn't he presented with one "grand narrative" after the other, with "certainties" shouted from the pulpit and from the mouths of revolutionaries, or whispered from the mouths of dreamers and armchair philosophers, and hadn't inevitable "progress" been promised to him as the indubitable rationale inbuilt in evolution and in the destiny of humanity? But all that lay bloodily shattered by two great wars and scores of small ones in the 20th century, and the being gifted with reason which man was supposed to be had shown that he was still more barbarian than ever. Heaven, in a hereafter or on the Earth, was guaranteed – how many times by how many religions? – and hell pervaded the world instead.

---

12. It is astonishing how, after the various incarnations of the totalitarian state (Nazism, Russian communism, Maoism...) which have scourged mankind, some of the brightest European thinkers (Claude Lévi-Strauss, Michel Foucault and their epigones), inheritors of the humanist tradition, were still capable of negating, against all life-experience and on an alleged basis of scientific materialism, the existence of the individual as such.

## Mind, Reason, Intellect

*A thought is an arrow shot at the truth; it can hit a point, but not cover the whole target ...*[13]

– Sri Aurobindo

*Western thought perished because of its certainties.*[14]

– Michel Winock

"Reason is the master of the nature of the human species,"[15] said the Mother, thus confirming that man is "the mental being" par excellence. "Reason using the intelligent will for the ordering of the inner and the outer life is undoubtedly the highest developed faculty of man at his present point of evolution; it is the sovereign, because the governing and self-governing faculty in the complexities of our human existence,"[16] wrote Sri Aurobindo. And: "It is a sovereign power by which man has become possessed of himself, student and master of his own forces, the godhead on which the other godheads in him have leaned for help in their ascent; it has been the Prometheus of the mythical parable, the helper, instructor, elevating friend, civiliser of mankind."[17] Seldom has somebody written more highly (and more beautifully) about reason. And as we have tried to show previously: reason (the mind, the intellect) has played a crucial role in the development of humanity by subjecting the whole civilisation of the Middle Ages to rational examination, by constructing an instrument for the rational investigation of nature,[18] and above all by developing the humanistic values

---

13. Sri Aurobindo: *Thoughts and Aphorisms,* in: *Essays Divine and Human,* p. 431. See also the section on "Mind" in Chapter 4: A First Sketch of Supermanhood.
14. Michel Winock: *Chronique des années soixante,* p. 62.
15. The Mother: *Questions and Answers 1957-58,* p. 101.
16. Sri Aurobindo: *The Human Cycle,* p. 102.
17. Id., p. 105.
18. "Natural philosophy" – what we now call "science" – however controversial

and the realisation of the individual, which have become the foundations of the global "family of man".

The value and the role of reason are therefore essential to a human humanity and deserve the highest esteem. Then why is reason devalued by all postmodern viewpoints? Why hold reason – once enthroned as the presiding deity of the French revolution as *la Déesse de la Raison*, the Goddess of Reason – responsible for the evils that befell humankind in the 20th century and for the uncertainty, anxiety and nihilism of the present time? The simple and far-reaching answer is, as already stated above, that the Western image of man and of reality was and remains fatefully defective. The "natural philosophy" of Galileo and Kepler has led to the recognition that Matter is the sole constituent of the universe; man, part of the universe, became nothing else than matter. Then, what is Mind? The high-wire intellectual acrobatics of the Western philosophers to formulate an answer to this question would look spectacularly grotesque – if they did not have such detrimental consequences. The outcome was that the materialists, positivists and reductionists labelled Mind an "epiphenomenon" of Matter. The word is indeed no more than a label and explains nothing. But it was inevitable that such a clown-like distortion of reality and of the image of man would one day have serious consequences and cause the kind of "postmodernist" confusion to which we are now subject.

> One dreamed and saw a gland write Hamlet, drink
>   At the Mermaid, capture immortality;
> A committee of hormones on the Aegean's brink
>   Composed the Iliad and the Odyssey.
>
> A thyroid, meditating almost nude
>   Under the Bo-tree, saw the eternal Light
> And, rising from its mighty solitude,
>   Spoke of the Wheel and the eightfold Path all right ...[19]

---

it may have become at present, seemed an almost miraculous discovery at the time of Galileo, Kepler and Newton.

19. Sri Aurobindo: *A Dream of Surreal Science*, in *Collected Poems*, p. 145.

"Western philosophies (including everyday common sense)", writes Glenn Ward, "revolve around an illusory metaphysics of presence. This can be found in myths about 'essence', 'meaning', 'cause', and 'self' – But such a presence is never purely present. Essential meanings are not just there: they are put there by the tools, knowledges and assumptions we use to look for them ... – All theories, arguments, texts, etc. rest on abstract systems of relationships. So they never touch down on the sure grounds of a preexisting and pure reality. – ... For poststructuralism (and so for postmodernism) there are no facts. There are only interpretations."[20] Nothing better than formulations like these, condensing scores of volumes of learned writing, tells us about the void the contemporary thinking Western human is living in. All essences – the Divine, the soul, the occult existences – are declared unknowable; everything is accidental, unexplainable in its origins (which are nothing but "abstract systems and relationships"), and without meaning in its becoming and destiny (for all "metanarratives" have proved to be nothing but hollow abstract systems); "there are no facts, only interpretations" by an epiphenomenon that is called reason, or mind, or the intellect, or the capacity for the human being to understand itself and the world. An epiphenomenon has imagined itself to be immortal. An epiphenomenon has created the airplane and computer. An epiphenomenon has constructed the theory of the Big Bang, the black hole and the Big Crunch. An epiphenomenon has discovered itself to be an epiphenomenon.

We, however, remain convinced that one metanarrative remains standing: the vision and world view of Sri Aurobindo and the Mother. If so, then we must also have an alternative explanation of what mind and reason really are. Passages on this theme abound in Sri Aurobindo and the Mother's writings – as there are also numerous ones on the fact that the mind has been totally misunderstood by the Western philosophers. True, reason was "the master of the human species". But even then there were gradations of existence below the rational mind as well as

---

20. Glenn Ward: *Postmodernism*, pp. 100-101.

above it. Existence is much more than a kind of abstraction, a verbal tool used by philosophers for their mental conjuring tricks. Existence is primarily the All, existent in and by itself; secondarily, existence is the ground of the All's infinitely varied manifestation as real as It is real, as concrete in the scale of its substances as It is concrete.[21] And in that picture, on that stair of the worlds, man has his place as a transitional being between the animal and the suprahuman species of the future. Man is the typical mental being, an embodiment on the Earth of the mental gradation in the universal manifestation. Keeping this in mind, let us see how Sri Aurobindo and the Mother defined Mind.

## 1. "Mind is not a faculty of knowledge"

- "Mind is an instrument of analysis and synthesis, but not of essential knowledge. Its function is to cut out something vaguely from the unknown Thing in itself and call this measurement or delimitation of it the whole, and again to analyse the whole into its parts which it regards as separate mental objects. It is only the parts and accidents that the Mind can see definitely and, after its own fashion, know. Of the whole its only definite idea is an assemblage of parts or a totality of properties and accidents. The whole not seen as a part of something else or in its own parts, properties and accidents is to the mind no more than a vague perception; only when it is analysed and put by itself as a separate constituted object, a totality in a larger totality, can Mind say to itself, 'This now I know.' And really it does not know. It knows only its own analysis of the object and the idea

---

21. "The Absolute manifests itself in two terms, a Being and a Becoming. The Being is the fundamental reality; the Becoming is an effectual reality: it is a dynamic power and result, a creative energy and working out of the Being, a constantly persistent yet mutable form, process, outcome of its immutable formless essence." (Sri Aurobindo: *The Life Divine*, p. 659)

it has formed of it by a synthesis of the separate parts and properties that it has seen."[22]

- "Mind by itself is incapable of ultimate certitude; whatever it believes, it can doubt; whatever it can affirm, it can deny; whatever it gets hold of, it can and does let go. That, if you like, is its freedom, noble right, privilege; it may be all you can say in its praise, but by these methods of mind you cannot hope (outside the reach of physical phenomena and hardly even there) to arrive at anything you can call an ultimate certitude. It is for this compelling reason that mentalising or enquiring about the Divine cannot by its own right bring the Divine."[23]

- "Reason is in its nature an imperfect light with a large but still restricted mission and that once it applies itself to life and action it becomes subject to what it studies and the servant and counsellor of the forces in whose obscure and ill-understood struggle it intervenes. It can by its nature be used and has always been used to justify any idea, theory of life, system of society or government, ideal of individual or collective action to which the will of man attaches itself for the moment or through the centuries. In philosophy it gives equally good reasons for monism and pluralism or for any halting-place between them, for the belief in Being or for the belief in Becoming, for optimism and pessimism, for activism and quietism. It can justify the most mystic religionism and the most positive atheism, get rid of God or see nothing else.

- "Ask it not to lean to one idea alone, but to make an eclectic combination or a synthetic harmony and it will satisfy you; only, there being any number of possible combinations or harmonies, it will equally well justify the one or the other and set up or throw down any one of them according as the spirit in man is attracted to or withdraws from it. For it is

---
22. Sri Aurobindo: *The Life Divine*, p. 127.
23. Sri Aurobindo: *Letters on Yoga*, p. 170.

## 4. Reason on Trial

really that which decides and the reason is only a brilliant servant and minister of this veiled and secret sovereign."[24]

- "Mind is in its essence a consciousness which measures, limits, cuts out forms of things from the indivisible whole and contains them as if each were a separate integer. Even with what exists only as obvious parts and fractions, Mind establishes this fiction of its ordinary commerce that they are things with which it can deal separately and not merely as aspects of a whole. For, even when it knows that they are not things in themselves, it is obliged to deal with them as if they were things in themselves; otherwise it could not subject them to its own characteristic activity.

- "It is this essential characteristic of Mind which conditions the workings of all its operative powers, whether conception, perception, sensation or the dealings of creative thought. It conceives, perceives, senses things as if rigidly cut out from a background or a mass and employs them as fixed units of the material given to it for creation or possession. All its action and enjoyment deal thus with wholes that form part of a greater whole, and these subordinate wholes again are broken up into parts which are also treated as wholes for the particular purposes they serve.[25] Mind may divide, multiply, add, subtract, but it cannot get beyond the limits of this mathematics. If it goes beyond and tries to conceive a real whole, it loses itself in a foreign element; it falls from its own firm ground into the ocean of the intangible."[26]

- "Man is limited in his consciousness by mind and even by a given range or scale of mind; what is below his mind, submental or mental but nether to his scale, readily seems to him subconscious or not distinguishable from complete inconscience; what is above it is to him superconscious and he is almost inclined to regard it as void of awareness, a sort

---

24. Sri Aurobindo: *The Human Cycle*, p. 121.
25. The reader familiar with the work of Ken Wilber will recognise here what Wilber calls "holons", a term he borrowed from Arthur Koestler.
26. Sri Aurobindo: *The Life Divine*, pp. 162-63.

of luminous Inconscience. Just as he is limited to a certain scale of sounds or of colours and what is above or below that scale is to him inaudible and invisible or at least indistinguishable, so is it with his scale of mental consciousness, confined at either extremity by an incapacity which marks his upper and his nether limit."

- "He has no sufficient means of communication even with the animal who is his mental congener, though not his equal, and he is even capable of denying mind or real consciousness to it because its modes are other and narrower than those with which in himself and his kind he is familiar; he can observe submental being from outside but cannot at all communicate with it or enter intimately into its nature. Equally the superconscious is to him a closed book which may well be filled only with empty pages."[27]

Therefore, in the view of Sri Aurobindo and the Mother: "First, we affirm an Absolute as the origin and support and secret Reality of all things. The Absolute Reality is indefinable and ineffable by mental thought and mental language; it is self-existent and self-evident to itself, as all absolutes are self-evident, but our mental affirmatives and negatives, whether taken separately or together, cannot limit or define it. But at the same time there is a spiritual consciousness, a spiritual knowledge, a knowledge by identity which can seize the Reality in its fundamental aspects and its manifested powers and figures. All that comes within this description and, if seen by this knowledge in its own truth or its occult meaning, can be regarded as an expression of the Reality and itself a reality."[28]

"The Absolute is in itself indefinable by reason, ineffable to the speech; it has to be approached through experience. It can be approached through an absolute negation of existence, as if it were itself a supreme Non-Existence, a mysterious infinite Nihil. It can be approached through an absolute affirmation of

---

27. Id., pp. 273-74.
28. Id., p. 658.

all the fundamentals of our own existence, through an absolute of Light and Knowledge, through an absolute of Love and Beauty, through an absolute of Force, through an absolute of peace or silence. It can be approached through an inexpressible absolute of being or of consciousness, or of power of being, or of delight of being, or through a supreme experience in which these things become inexpressibly one; for we can enter into such an ineffable state and, plunged into it as if into a luminous abyss of existence, we can reach a superconscience which may be described as the gate of the Absolute."[29]

In conclusion: "All our illusions and errors arise from a limited separative awareness which creates unrealities or misconceives the Real." – "It might almost be said that no mental statement of things can be altogether true; it is not Truth bodied, pure and nude, but a draped figure, – often it is only the drapery that is visible." – "It is always the business of man the thinker to know. He may not be able by mental means to know the essentiality of the Ignorance or of anything in the universe in the sense of defining it, because the mind can only know things in that sense by their signs, characters, forms, properties, functionings, relations to other things, not in their occult self-being and essence. But we can pursue farther and farther, clarify more and more accurately our observation of the phenomenal character and operation of the Ignorance until we get the right revealing word, the right indicating sense of the thing and so come to know it, not by intellect but by vision and experience of the truth, by realising the truth in our own being. The whole process of man's highest intellectual knowledge is through this mental manipulation and discrimination to the point where the veil is broken and he can see; at the end spiritual knowledge comes in to help us to become what we see, to enter into the light in which there is no Ignorance."[30]

---

29. Id., p. 476.
30. Id., pp. 481, 599 and 488.

## 2. Mind is Substance, Thoughts are Entities

"The mind is an instrument of formation, of organisation and action. Why? The mind gives a form to the thoughts. This power of formation forms mental entities whose life is independent of the mind that has formed them – they act as beings that are at least semi-independent. One can form a thought which then travels, goes out to someone, spreads the idea it contains. There is a mental substance just as there is a physical substance, and on [its own] plane the mind can emanate innumerable forms."[31]

- "We regard thought as a thing separate from existence, abstract, unsubstantial, different from reality, something which appears one knows not whence and detaches itself from objective reality in order to observe, understand and judge it; for so it seems and therefore is to our all-dividing, all-analysing mentality. The first business of Mind is to render 'discrete', to make fissures much more than to discern, and so it has made this paralysing fissure between thought and reality."[32]

- "For the mind is an instrument of action and formation, not an instrument of knowledge. It is creating forms every moment. Thoughts are forms and have an individual life, independent of their originator; sent out by him into the world, they move in it towards the realisation of their own purpose of existence … If there is a sufficient will-power in your thought-form, if it is a well-built formation, it will arrive at its own realisation. But between the formation and the realisation there is a certain lapse of time … and it happens very often that when the result does come, you have ceased to desire it or care for it."[33]

- "For man's mentality is also a part of Nature; his mentality

---

31. *Words of the Mother,* CWM 15, p. 329.
32. Sri Aurobindo: *The Life Divine,* pp. 129-30.
33. The Mother: *Questions and Answers 1929-31,* pp. 50-51.

is even the most important, if not the largest part of his nature. It is, we may say, Nature become partly conscious of her own laws and forces, conscious of her struggle of progression and inspired with the conscious will to impose a higher and higher law on her own processes of life and being. In subhuman life there is a vital and physical struggle, but no mental conflict. Man is subjected to this mental conflict and is therefore at war not only with others but with himself; and because he is capable of this war with himself, he is also capable of that which is denied to the animal, of an inner evolution, a progression from higher to higher type, a constant self-transcending."[34]

- "The error comes from thinking that your thoughts are your own and that you are their maker and if you do not create thoughts (i.e. think), there will be none. A little observation ought to show that you are not manufacturing your own thoughts, but rather thoughts occur in you. Thoughts are born, not made – like poets, according to the proverb. Of course, there is a sort of labour and effort when you try to produce or else to think on a certain subject, but that is a concentration, for making thoughts come up, come in, come down, as the case may be, and fit themselves together. The idea that you are shaping the thoughts or fitting them together is an egoistic delusion ..."

- "Thoughts, ideas, happy inventions etc., etc., are always wandering about (in thought waves or otherwise) seeking a mind that may embody them. One mind takes, looks, rejects – another takes, looks, accepts. Two different minds catch the same thought-form or thought-wave, but the mental activities being different make different results out of them. Or it comes to one and he does nothing, then it walks off, crying 'O this unready animal!' and goes to another who promptly annexes it and it settles into expression with a joyous bubble of inspiration, illumination or enthusiasm

---

34. Sri Aurobindo: *The Human Cycle,* p. 418.

of original discovery or creation and the recipient cries proudly, 'I, I have done this.' Ego, sir! You are the recipient, the conditioning medium, if you like – nothing more! ..."

- "First of all these thought-waves, thought-seeds or thought-forms, or whatever they are, are of different values and come from different planes of consciousness. Even the same thought-substance can take higher or lower vibrations according to the plane of consciousness through which the thoughts come in (e.g. thinking mind, vital mind, physical mind, subconscient mind) or the power of consciousness which catches them and pushes them into one man or another. Moreover there is a stuff of mind in each man and the incoming thought uses that for shaping itself or translating itself (transcribing we usually call it), but the stuff is finer or coarser, stronger or weaker etc., etc., in one mind than in another. Also there is a mind-energy actual or potential in each which differs and this mind-energy in its recipience of the thought can be luminous or obscure, *sattwic, rajasic* or *tamasic* with consequences that vary in each case."[35]

- "The human mind is like a town square, accessible on all sides, and in this square things come and go, and pass by each other in all directions. Some settle there, and they are not always the best. To obtain control over that crowd is the most difficult kind of control possible. Just try to control the thoughts entering your mind and you will see! You will see to what a degree you have to be watchful, like a sentinel, with the eyes of the mind wide open, and how you have to keep up an extremely clear distinction between the ideas in agreement with your aspirations and those who are not. And you must keep order every minute in that public place where avenues meet from all sides, so that people do not run into each other. It's a big job."[36]

---

35. Nirodbaran: *Correspondence with Sri Aurobindo*, pp. 357, 358 and 362.
36. The Mother: *Questions and Answers 1950-51*, p. 335.

## 4. Reason on Trial

This knowledge of what the Mind really is is based on centuries-old yogic traditions of patient observation and discernment. The difference from the Western epistemological disarray, responsible for the shaky foundations of all Western philosophical schools, is obvious. It is, of course closely connected with the difference in interpretation between the Western and Eastern world view and idea of Reality. Constructions erected on the shaky foundations of the Western philosophical premises had to collapse sooner or later. That it collapses now makes its timing perfectly synchronous with the moment when the world is taking its momentous turn towards a new, divine world order. And not only is the collapse happening at this moment: it is part of the transitional event.

According to the Mother a consciousness higher than the human rational mind has recently been established in the atmosphere of the Earth and is active here. She called it, after Sri Aurobindo, the supramental consciousness and said that it would embody first in the overman and then as the superman. This does not mean that the rational mind is of no use any longer. For a long time to come it will remain the highest attainable consciousness of the human mass; should the rational mind be forsaken, this mass would without doubt fall back into the horrors of its animality, present-day examples of which are not lacking. Besides, a clear mind is necessary to gain access to the realms beyond it, something many practitioners of yoga are unaware of in their ignorance or forget in their premature pride.

"If you do not become perfectly and luminously logical and rational, how can you hope to become a candidate for the next higher stage even?"[37] asked Sri Aurobindo. "One has to be reasonable even in spirituality."[38] And the Mother warned: "There are people who try to transform their body even before having transformed their intellect, and this produces a total discrepancy, it unbalances them completely. One must first transform one's thought, one's whole mind, one's whole mental activity,

---

37. Nirodbaran: op.cit. p. 325.
38. Nirodbaran: *Talks with Sri Aurobindo* I, p. 72.

and organise it with the higher knowledge. At the same time one must transform one's character, all the movements of the vital, all impulses, all vital reactions. Finally, when both these things are done, up to a certain point at least, one can begin to think of transforming the cells of one's body. But one does not begin at the end: one must begin at the beginnings."[39]

Sri Aurobindo and the Mother never denigrated the rational mind, the intellect, the element that makes man specifically human. As any other level of the scale of being, the rational mind is an essential element in the total manifestation; constituting the proper characteristic of the human species, it is also the instrument that makes the transition from the lower to the higher hemisphere possible. "The rational or intellectual man is not the last and highest ideal of manhood, nor would a rational society be the last and highest expression of the possibilities of an aggregate human life, – unless indeed we give to the word, reason, a wider meaning than it now possesses and include in it the combined wisdom of all our powers of knowledge, those which stand below and above the understanding and logical mind as well as this strictly rational part of our nature. The Spirit that manifests itself in man and dominates secretly the phases of his development, is greater and profounder than his intellect and drives towards a perfection that cannot be shut in by the arbitrary construction of the human reason. Meanwhile the intellect performs its function; it leads man to the gates of a greater self-consciousness and places him with unbandaged eyes on that wide threshold where a more luminous Angel has to take him by the hand."[40] "Mind is not a separate entity", writes Sri Aurobindo also, "but has all Supermind behind it and it is Supermind that creates with Mind only as its final individualising operation."[41] It is Supermind – the Truth-Consciousness, the Unity-Consciousness – that manifests the cosmos and that supports it at every moment of its existence and evolution; without this omniscient, omnipotent and omnipresent Consciousness

---

39. The Mother: *Question and Answers* 1955, p. 204.
40. Sri Aurobindo: *The Human Cycle,* p. 105.
41. Sri Aurobindo: *The Life Divine,* p. 190.

behind it, the cosmos could not exist or would be utter chaos.[42] "This Supermind in its conscious vision not only contains all the forms of itself which its conscious force creates, but it pervades them as an indwelling Presence and a self-revealing Light. It is present, even though concealed, in every form and force of the universe; it is that which determines sovereignly and spontaneously form, force and functioning; it limits the variations it compels; it gathers, disperses, modifies the energy which it uses; and all this is done in accord with the first laws that its self-knowledge has fixed in the very birth of the form, at the very starting-point of the force. It is seated within everything as the Lord in the heart of all existences, – he who turns them on as an engine by the power of his Maya; it is within them and embraces them as the divine Seer who variously disposed and ordained objects, each rightly according to the thing that it is, from years sempiternal.

"Each thing in Nature, therefore, whether animate or inanimate, mentally self-conscious or not self-conscious, is governed in its being and in its operations by an indwelling Vision and Power, to us subconscient or inconscient because we are not conscious of it, but not inconscient to itself, rather profoundly and universally conscient. Therefore each thing seems to do the works of intelligence, even without possessing intelligence, because it obeys, whether subconsciously as in the plant and animal or half-consciously as in man, the real-idea of the divine Supermind within it."[43]

Sri Aurobindo and the Mother knew that the Mind could not remain the dominant principle of humanity and that it would be surpassed. Sri Aurobindo saw the first signs of this at

---

42. See the chapter called "The Divine Maya" in *The Life Divine*, p. 112 ff. – It is painful to read time and again how childish the notions of some of the most famous scientists are when they write about "the mind of God". They always seem to think that God's mind is something like their own human mind, although perhaps a little more powerful. If science takes years of intensive training and is not accessible to everybody then it is reasonable to suppose that knowledge of "the mind of God" may demand some training too.
43. Sri Aurobindo: *The Life Divine,* pp. 135-36.

the time he was writing the *Arya*, i.e. during and just after the First World War. "In the present time itself, after an age of triumphant intellectuality and materialism, we can see evidences of this natural process, – a return towards inner self-discovery, an inner seeking and thinking, a new attempt at mystic experience, a groping after the inner self, a reawakening to some sense of the truth and power of the spirit begins to manifest itself; man's search after his self and soul and a deeper truth of things tends to revive and resume its lost force and to give a fresh life to the old creeds, erect new faiths or develop independently of sectarian religions. The intellect itself, having reached near to the natural limits of the capacity of physical discovery, having touched its bedrock and found that it explains nothing more than the outer process of Nature, has begun, still tentatively and hesitatingly, to direct an eye of research on the deeper secrets of the mind and the life-force and on the domain of the occult which it had rejected *a priori*, in order to know what there may be in it that is true."[44]

"At present mankind is undergoing an evolutionary crisis in which is concealed a choice of its destiny; for a stage has been reached in which the human mind has achieved in certain directions an enormous development while in others it stands arrested and bewildered and can no longer find its way", wrote Sri Aurobindo in *The Life Divine*. "A structure of the external life has been raised up by man's ever active mind and life-will, a structure of an unmanageable hugeness and complexity, for the service of his mental, vital, physical claims and urges, a complex political, social, administrative, economic, cultural machinery, an organised collective means for his intellectual, sensational, aesthetic and material satisfaction. Man has created a system of civilisation which has become too big for his limited mental capacity and understanding and his still more limited spiritual and moral capacity to utilise and manage, a too dangerous servant of his blundering ego and its appetites. For no greater seeing mind, no intuitive soul of knowledge has yet come to his surface

---
44. Id., pp. 867-68.

of consciousness which could make this basic fullness of life a condition for the free growth of something that exceeded it.

"This new fullness of the means of life might be, by its power for a release from the incessant unsatisfied stress of his economic and physical needs, an opportunity for the full pursuit of other and greater aims surpassing the material existence, for the discovery of a higher truth and good and beauty, for the discovery of a greater and diviner spirit which would intervene and use life for a higher perfection of the being: but it is being used instead for the multiplication of new wants and an aggressive expansion of the collective ego. At the same time Science has put at his disposal many potencies of the universal Force and has made the life of humanity materially one; but what uses this universal Force is a little human individual or communal ego with nothing universal in its light of knowledge or its movements, no inner sense or power which would create in this physical drawing together of the human world a true life-unity, a mental unity or a spiritual oneness ...

"The evolution of the human mind and life must necessarily lead towards an increasing universality; but on a basis of ego and segmenting and dividing mind this opening to the universal can only create a vast pullulation of unaccorded ideas and impulses, a surge of enormous powers and desires, a chaotic mass of unassimilated and intermixed mental, vital and physical material of a larger existence which, because it is not taken up by a creative harmonising light of the Spirit, must welter in a universalised confusion and discord out of which it is impossible to build a greater harmonic life. Man has harmonised life in the past by organised ideation and limitation; he has created societies based on fixed ideas or fixed customs, a fixed cultural system or an organised life-system, each with its own order; the throwing of all these into the melting-pot of a more and more intermingling life and a pouring in of ever new ideas and motives and facts and possibilities call for a new, a greater consciousness to meet and master the increasing potentialities of existence and harmonise them. Reason and Science can only help by standardising, by fixing everything into an artificially arranged and mechanised unity of material life. A greater whole-being, whole-knowledge, whole-power is needed to weld all into a greater unity of whole-life."[45]

---

45. Id., pp. 1053 ff.

# 5
# Science, Scientism, Modern Technology

> *We must look existence in the face in whatever aspect it confronts us and be strong to find within as well as behind it the Divine.*[1]
>
> – SRI AUROBINDO
>
> *And tell me: is that story, sung by mystics and sages the world over, any crazier than the scientific materialistic story, which is that the entire sequence is a tale told by an idiot, full of sound and fury, signifying absolutely nothing? Listen very carefully: just which of those two stories actually sounds totally insane?*[2]
>
> – KEN WILBER

Science is certainly one of the great accomplishments, not to say the main accomplishment, of reason in the centuries subsequent to the Middle Ages. It has changed the world to an enormous degree and seems to be triumphant everywhere. And not only has it changed our world: it is considered by many to be the only reliable instrument and even the ultimate source of knowledge.

---

1. Sri Aurobindo: *Essays in Philosophy and Yoga*, p. 191.
2. Ken Wilber: *A Brief History of Everything*, p. 43.

## 1. Is Science the Dominating Paradigm Today?

For many of the best-known scientists, philosophers and other kinds of learned and looked-up-to people (medical doctors, psychologists, professors, generals, captains of industry, philosophers, etc.) who are influential in shaping the present worldview, science is the dominant paradigm. They are quite supercilious if not aggressive about it and send the doubters of their reductionist-positivist-materialistic paradigm ruthlessly to the sidelines. At many universities and think tanks, at many enterprises and in many professions it is simply not safe to question the radical scientific outlook.

One example of this outlook is the January 1998 special issue of *Time*, titled *The New Age of Discovery: A Celebration of Mankind's Exploration of the Unknown*. A promising, wide-ranging subject matter indeed, attractive to anyone concerned with the problems and expectations of what in 1998 was still the coming millennium. A few quotations will show better than any comment what sort of mental attitudes were offered to the reader.

- "In the past decade or so evolutionary theory has yielded a mind-blowing discovery: it has pried open the neatly-arranged toolbox that is our mind. Just as *Gray's Anatomy* laid bare the human frame, so Darwinian scientists are beginning to write the owner-occupier's manual to that hitherto most recondite of mysteries: human nature. Yes, human nature does exist and it is universal. Our minds and brains, just like our bodies, have been honed by natural selection to solve the problems faced by our ancestors over the past two million years. Just as every normal human hand has a precision-engineered opposable thumb for plucking, so every normal human mind enters the world bristling with highly specialized problem-solving equipment. And these capacities come on stream during development as surely as the toddler's first faltering steps or the adolescent's acne and ecstasy ... All this apparent design has come about without a designer. No purpose, no goals, no blueprints. Natural selection is simply about genes replicating themselves down the generations ..." (Helena Cronin: "The Evolution of Evolution", p. 53)

- "Evolution depends upon errors in reproduction ... There is nothing mysterious about evolution. It is no more than genetics plus time." (Steve Jones: "Going Nowhere, Very Fast", p. 54)

- "There is good reason to believe that consciousness is not only caused by neurobiological states but actually is these neurobiological states. As Francis Crick, co-discoverer of the molecular structure of DNA in 1953, has suggested: '"You", your joys and your sorrows, your memories and your ambitions, your sense of personal identity and free will, are in fact no more than the behaviour of a vast assembly of nerve cells and their associated molecules.' And yet something else may be needed – not some divine spark or soul, but some as yet unknown aspect of brain activity ..." (Steve Jones, ibid.)

It should in fairness be said that the editors of *Time* gave a chance for other voices to be heard too, but the general trend of the issue is predominantly techno-scientific in accordance with the reigning paradigm of materialism.

Here are some other examples of scientism picked more or less at random. Charles Panati, former science editor of *Newsweek*, writes in his book *Breakthroughs*: "Fifty years ago, Sigmund Freud predicted that every mental event would one day be traced to chemical reactions in the brain. Today, scientists are proving him right. Not that their 1960s' analogy of the brain as a complex computer is wrong, but scientists are learning that a more fundamental and fruitful approach to understanding the brain's functions is to view it as a giant chemistry set. For the first time scientists are measuring minuscule amounts of brain chemicals, tagging them and tracing their intricate pathways. Memory, concentration, fear – even aggression – have all recently been identified as chemical events", (p. 136) – "We can be both smugly pleased and profoundly disappointed that such emotions as joy, love, aggression, and fear are firmly rooted in the chemical soil of the brain. The fact may make us seem less human, but at the same time more wondrous in design." (p. 142) – "Dream images, [Harvard psychiatrists Allan Hobson and Robert Mc Carleay] contend, amount to little more than the efforts of the logical brain trying to make sense of the body's electrical impulses it receives while you're sleeping." (p. 157)

On 28 November 2000, the *New Indian Express* carried an article under the title: "Love or hate, it's all in the brain". "Why do we love some people and hate others? Why do we befriend some, despise others? Well, bless or blame the brain for how we react to people and to the environment around us ... In fact, the brain establishes one million connections every second. But the brain decides which connections to retain and which to discard ... While the size and shape of the brain has remained the same since the Stone Age, man has been able to change the very face of the earth using his mental ability. This is because we are making our brains smarter by establishing new links and allowing the neurons to chat in a language that gives meaning to our actions."

Richard Dawkins, the leading proponent of sociobiology and author of some best-selling books like *The Selfish Gene* and *The Blind Watchmaker*, writes in *River out of Eden* (1995): "The universe we observe has precisely the properties we should expect if there is, at bottom, no design, no purpose, no evil and no good, nothing but blind, pitiless indifference ... DNA neither cares nor knows. DNA just is. And we dance to its music." Francis Crick is quoted above; here follows an opinion from his co-discoverer of the structure of DNA, James Watson. The journalist of the French magazine *Courrier International* first writes: "He [James Watson] has proposed to modify the genetic code not of one single individual but of the future generations." Then he quotes Watson's words: "Some will have to show the courage to intervene in the germinal [i.e. genetic and therefore definitive] line without being sure of the result. Besides (and nobody dares to say this): if we could create better humans through an addition of genes, deriving from plants or animals,

## 5. Science, Scientism, Modern Technology

why not take the chance? What is the problem?"[3] If there were an award for ideas of science-gone-bonkers, this pronouncement by a scientist of worldwide renown would be one of the chief contenders.

It goes without saying that this small string of quotations is only meant to be illustrative. For the full picture we turn to Huston Smith: "The reductionistic moment has not abated. Beginning with consciousness, we find Daniel Dennett telling us that 'materialism in one form or another is the reigning orthodoxy among philosophers of the mind' and Carl Sagan saying in his *The Dragons of Eden* that his fundamental premise about the brain is that its workings – what we sometimes call 'mind' – 'are a consequence of its anatomy and physiology and nothing more' ... 'Biologists', Harold Morowitz, professor of molecular biophysics and biochemistry at Yale tells us, 'have been moving relentlessly toward hardcore materialism.' Francis Crick [him again!], co-discoverer of DNA, agrees: 'The ultimate aim of the modern movement in biology is to explain all biology in terms of physics and chemistry.' And Morowitz again: As physiologists study the activity of living cells in terms of processes carried out by organelles of living cells and other subcellular entities, the study of life at all levels, from social to molecular behaviour, has in modern times relied on reductionism as the chief explanatory concept."[4]

Nevertheless, there is obviously more than scientism (i.e. dogmatic science) in the contemporary world. The adherents

---

3. *Le Courrier International*, 21 December 2000, p. 48.
4. Huston Smith: *Beyond the Post-Modern Mind*, pp. 201-2. In its issue of 5 February 2001, *Newsweek* carries a column on science with the title "Searching for the God Within" (Really?) and the eye-catcher "The way our brains are wired may explain the origin of religious beliefs." (Really!) The column announces that Dr. Andrew Newberg and the late Dr. Eugene d'Aquili have named a new field "neurotheology". "The human brain has been genetically wired to encourage religious beliefs", they have concluded. "As long as our brain is wired as it is", says Newberg, "God will not go away." Writes Sharon Begley, *Newsweek*'s science editor: "Neuro-theology at least suggests that spiritual experiences are no more meaningful than, say, the fear the brain is hard-wired to feel in response to a strange noise at night."

of the main religions, Hinduism, Buddhism, Islam and Christianity, are counted in the hundreds of millions. The Pope draws crowds of hundreds of thousands; in the year 2001 the participants in the Kumbha Mela, at Allahabad in India, the greatest human gathering ever, numbered seventy million; tens of thousands have marched on the White House in Washington for one Christian cause or another; and tens of thousands perform the *haj*, the pilgrimage to Mecca year after year. In France one talks about "the Buddhist wave"[5], for in the country of Descartes (*Descartes, c'est la France!*) there are now 600,000 Buddhists, half of them Asiatics, the other half native Frenchmen. In The Netherlands, a much smaller country than France, there are 250,000 Buddhists. The presence and influence of Freemasonry in Western society is undiminished. The New Age movement has spread its rainbow branches all over the globe. Occultism has always been very much alive as a subterranean current in the European landscape of the mind, even in the Age of Reason and the positivist 19th century; today it is experiencing a general revival to which the countless publications in the bookstores from 1970 onwards bear testimony.

One telling example in support of this: on 7 December 2000, *L'Express* published an enquiry about "The astonishing influence of the astrologers". There are no less than 10,000 astrologers in France, and one Frenchman out of ten consults them. They are asked for advice by many of the prominent people in the land, ambassadors as well as financiers and politicians. It is known that Charles de Gaulle, Ronald and Nancy Reagan, Boris Yeltsin, François Mitterand and king Juan Carlos of Spain have sought astrological advice. Most of the politicians in India regularly consult their favourite astrologer.

Science, long presumed to be unshakable because based on mathematics, is more and more called into question. In this context it is of primary importance to recall that the giants of science never put on the strait-jacket of scientism. Ken Wilber has done yeoman service to all interested in the topic covered

---

5. *L'Express,* 24 October 1996, p. 48.

in this section by selecting *Quantum Questions: Mystic writings of the world's great physicists*. There we read for instance the following words of a theoretical physicist of the calibre of Werner Heisenberg (1901-1976): "1. Modern science, in its beginnings, was characterised by a conscious modesty; it made statements about strictly limited relations that *are only valid within the framework of these limitations*. 2. *This modesty was largely lost during the nineteenth century*. Physical knowledge was considered to make assertions about nature as a whole. Physics wished to turn philosopher, and the demand was voiced from many quarters that all true philosophers must be scientific. 3. Today [this was first published in 1971] physics is undergoing a basic change, the most characteristic trait of which is a return to its original self-limitation. 4. The philosophic content of science is only preserved if science is conscious of its limits. Great discoveries of the properties of individual phenomena are possible only if the nature of the phenomena is not generalised *à priori*. Only by leaving open the question of the ultimate essence of a body, of matter, of energy, etc., can physics reach an understanding of the individual properties of the phenomena that we designate by these concepts, an understanding which alone may lead us to real philosophical insight." (p. 73, emphasis in the text) A "runaway national best-seller" in the USA was John Horgan's remarkable book *The End of Science*. Horgan is a former senior writer at *Scientific American* (and has now published the no less remarkable *The Undiscovered Brain*). Two brief quotations from his contribution to the aforementioned issue of *Time* will have to suffice. "I suspect that the more intelligent or aware or enlightened we become – whether through drugs or meditation or genetic engineering or artificial intelligence – the more we will be astonished, awestruck, dumbfounded by consciousness, and life, and the whole universe, regardless of the power of our scientific explanations ... Consciousness would only be truly understood not from the outside but from the inside, not through science but through experience." (pp. 266-67, emphasis in the text) And: "Consciousness is arguably the most philosophically resonant problem posed by the mind, but it is also arguably the most intractable and impractical problem ... Given their poor record to date, I fear that neuroscience, psychology, psychiatry, and other fields addressing the mind might be bumping up against fundamental limits of science. Scientists may never completely succeed in healing, replicating, or explaining the human mind. Our minds may always remain, to some extent, undiscovered." (pp. 3 and 10)

Let us return now to Sri Aurobindo: "The attempts of the positive critical reason to dissect the phenomena of the religious life sound to men of spiritual experience like the prattle of a child who is trying to shape into the mould of his own habitual notions the life of adults or the blunders of an ignorant mind which thinks fit to criticise patronisingly or adversely the labours of a profound thinker or a great scientist. At the best even this futile labour can extract, can account for only the externals of the things it attempts to explain; the spirit is missed, the inner matter is left out, and as a result of that capital omission even the account of the externals is left without real truth and has only an apparent correctness."[6]

## 2. Sri Aurobindo, the Mother, and Science

In an article published in the *Arya* in 1918, Sri Aurobindo wrote: "Admit, – for it is true, – that the age of which materialism was the portentous offspring and in which it had figured first as petulant rebel and aggressive thinker, then as a grave and strenuous preceptor of mankind, has been by no means a period of mere error, calamity and degeneration, but rather a most powerful creative epoch of humanity. Examine impartially its results. Not only has it immensely widened and filled in the knowledge of the race and accustomed it to a great patience of research, scrupulosity, accuracy, – if it has done that only in one large sphere of inquiry, it has still prepared for the extension of

---

6. Sri Aurobindo: *The Human Cycle,* p. 129.

## 5. Science, Scientism, Modern Technology

the same curiosity, intellectual rectitude, power for knowledge to other and higher fields, – not only has it with an unexampled force and richness of invention brought and put into our hands, for much evil, but also for much good, discoveries, instruments, practical powers, conquests, conveniences which, however we may declare their insufficiency for our higher interests, yet few of us would care to relinquish, but it has also, paradoxical as that might at first seem, strengthened man's idealism. On the whole, it has given him a kindlier hope and humanised his nature ... Now that we have founded rigorously our knowledge of the physical, we can go forward with a much firmer step to a more open, secure and luminous repossession of mental and psychic knowledge. Even spiritual truths are likely to gain from it,[7] not a loftier or more penetrating, – that is with difficulty possible, – but an ampler light and fuller self-expression."[8] This passage is typical of Sri Aurobindo and the Mother who never forgot that everything is the Brahman and that therefore everything has its value and significance; yet, they also saw the big picture and knew where to place everything in the general framework. They were the advocates of a "spiritual realism" for whom "the touch of Earth is always reinvigorating to the son of Earth, even when he seeks a supraphysical knowledge. It may even be said that the supraphysical can only be really mastered in its fullness ... when we keep our feet firmly on the physical."[9] And was it not their aim to transform Matter, a process that necessarily demands a continuous attention to it and a direct knowledge of it? But: "Neither the laws nor the possibilities of physical Nature can be entirely known unless we know also the laws and possibilities of supraphysical Nature; therefore the development of new and the recovery of old mental and psychic sciences have to follow

---

7. Cf. Sri Aurobindo's statement: "We [he and the Mother] do not found ourselves on faith alone, but on a great ground of knowledge which we have been developing and testing all our lives. I think I can say that I have been testing day and night for years upon years more scrupulously than any scientist his theory or his method on the physical plane." (*On Himself*, pp. 468-69)
8. Reprinted in Sri Aurobindo: *Essays in Philosophy and Yoga*, pp. 185 ff.
9. Sri Aurobindo: *The Life Divine*, p. 11.

upon the perfection of our physical knowledge, and that new era is already beginning to open upon us. *But the perfection of the physical sciences was a prior necessity and had to be the first field for the training of the mind of man in his new endeavour to know Nature and possess his world.*"[10] One would be mistaken if one thought that Sri Aurobindo, "mystic and poet", had no notion of science. Until now this aspect of his writings has been almost entirely overlooked, possibly because his commentators were but little scientifically inclined. Once again a few passages from his works will have to do.

- "Not only in the one final conception, but in the great line of its general results Knowledge, by whatever path it is followed, tends to become one. Nothing can be more remarkable and suggestive than the extent to which modern Science confirms in the domain of Matter the conceptions and even the very formulae of language which were arrived at, by a very different method, in the Vedanta, – the original Vedanta, not the schools of metaphysical philosophy, but of the *Upanishads*. And these, on the other hand, often reveal their full significance, their richer contents only when they are viewed in the new light shed by the discoveries of modern Science, – for instance, that Vedantic expression which describes things in the Cosmos as one seed arranged by the universal Energy in multitudinous forms. Significant, especially, is the drive of Science towards the Vedic idea of the one essence with its many becomings ... *It will be evident that essential Matter is a thing non-existent to the senses and only, like the Pradhana of the Sankyas, a conceptual form of substance; and in fact the point is increasingly reached where only an arbitrary distinction in thought divides form of substance from form of energy.*"[11] This was written before the formulation of the theory of quantum mechanics.

- "Spiritual experience tells us that there is a Reality which

---

10. Sri Aurobindo: *The Human Cycle,* p. 78 (emphasis added).
11. Sri Aurobindo: *The Life Divine,* p. 14 (emphasis added).

## 5. Science, Scientism, Modern Technology

supports and pervades all things as the Cosmic Self and Spirit, can be discovered by the individual even here in the terrestrial embodiment as his own self and spirit, and is, at its summits and in its essence, and infinite and eternal Being, Consciousness and Bliss [Sachchidananda] of existence. But what we seem to see as the source and beginning of the material universe is just the contrary – it wears to us the aspect of a Void, an infinite of Non-Existence, and indeterminate Inconscient, an insensitive blissless Zero out of which everything has yet to come.

"When it begins to move, evolve, create, it puts on the appearance of an inconscient Energy which delivers existence out of the Void in the form of an infinitesimal fragmentation, the electron – or perhaps some still more impalpable minute unit, then the atom, the molecule, and out of this fragmentation builds up a formed and concrete universe in the void of its infinite. Yet we see that this unconscious Energy does at every step the works of a vast and minute Intelligence fixing and combining every possible device to prepare, manage and work out the paradox and miracle of Matter and the awakening of a life and a spirit in Matter; existence grows out of the Void, consciousness emerges and increases out of the Inconscient, an ascending urge towards pleasure, happiness, delight, divine bliss and ecstasy is inexplicably born out of an insensitive Nihil ..."[12]

Sri Aurobindo's epic poem *Savitri*, on which he was working almost till the day he passed away, contains many passages that are pure science but formulated in the mantric lines of the seer. The following is one of these passages:

> At first was only an etheric Space:
> Its huge vibrations circled round and round
> Housing some unconceived initiative:
> Upheld by a supreme original Breath
> Expansion and contraction's mystic act

---

12. Sri Aurobindo: *The Human Cycle*, p. 169.

> Created touch and friction in the void,
> Into abstract emptiness brought clash and clasp:
> Parent of an expanding universe
> In a matrix of disintegrating force,
> By spending it conserved an endless sum.
> On the heart of Space it kindled a viewless Fire
> That, scattering worlds as one might scatter seeds,
> Whirled out the luminous order of the stars.
> An ocean of electric Energy
> Formlessly formed its strange wave-particles
> Constructing by their dance this solid scheme,
> Its mightiness in the atom shut to rest;
> Masses were forged or feigned and visible shapes;
> Light flung the photon's swift revealing spark
> And showed, in the minuteness of its flash
> Imaged, this cosmos of apparent things.
> Thus has been made this real impossible world,
> An obvious miracle or convincing show.[13]

As the Mother said: "If [science] moves in a very definite direction, if it progresses sufficiently, if it does not come to a halt on the way, the scientists will find the same thing the mystics have found, that the religious people have found, that everybody has found, because there is only one thing to be found. There are not two, there is only one."[14] The Mother generally spoke very highly of science. "I must say that the scientific method is a marvellous discipline. What is remarkable is that the method recommended by the Buddha to get rid of the desires and the illusion of the world, is also one of the most marvellous disciplines ever known on the earth. They are at the two opposite ends, they are both excellent. Those who follow the one or the other in all sincerity truly prepare themselves for the yoga. A small something somewhere will suffice to make

---

13. Sri Aurobindo: *Savitri*, p. 155. See also in *Questions and Answers 1953*, pp. 67-68, the revealing passage of a conversation on science Sri Aurobindo had in 1925 or 1926 with Pavitra, the French disciple who was a scientist with a degree from the *École polytechnique* in Paris.
14. The Mother: *Questions and Answers 1953*, p. 82.

## 5. Science, Scientism, Modern Technology

them leave their rather narrow viewpoint on the one side or the other, and allow them to reach an integrality which will lead them to the supreme Truth and mastery."[15]

In the 1950s, the Mother said several times that she foresaw the possibility that science and spirituality would join. Fundamentally there is nothing to prevent this, as both are in search of one thing only: the Truth. The reason of the divergence of science and spirituality was no other than the narrow dogmatism of the Catholic Church at the time of the post-Renaissance. The burning at the stake of Giordano Bruno and the condemnation of Galileo Galilei will forever remain emblematic of Rome's sectarian, dogmatic attitude. "It is not impossible to foresee the development in which the two will unite in a very deep and close understanding of the essential truth,"[16] said the Mother in 1957. "One step more and [the scientists] will enter into the Truth,"[17] she said a few months later.

Unfortunately, the hardened position of scientism, which had become a Church in its own right, would make the Mother gradually adopt the position which Sri Aurobindo had formulated in a letter to a disciple some twenty years earlier: "The physicist is not likely to be the bridge-builder." He explained in another letter: "The physical scientists have their own field with its own instruments and standards. To apply the same tests to phenomena of a different kind is as foolish as to apply physical tests to spiritual truth. One can't dissect God or see the soul under a microscope. So also the subjection of disembodied spirits or even of psychophysical phenomena to tests and standards valid only for material phenomena is a most false and unsatisfactory method. Moreover, the physical scientist is for the most part resolved not to admit what cannot be neatly packed and labelled and docketed in his own system and its formulas."[18]

On the whole, science has two important accomplishments

---

15. The Mother: *Questions and Answers 1955*, pp. 364-65.
16. The Mother: *Questions and Answers 1957-58*, p. 109.
17. Id., p. 239.
18. Sri Aurobindo: *Letters on Yoga*, p. 201.

to its credit. One is *the unification of mankind.* "Science pursuing its cold and even way has made discoveries which have served on one side a practical humanitarianism, on the other supplied monstrous weapons to egoism and mutual destruction; it has made possible a gigantic efficiency of organisation which has been used on one side for the economic and social amelioration of the nations and on the other for turning each into a colossal battering-ram of aggression, ruin and slaughter. It has given rise on the one side to a large rationalistic and altruistic humanitarianism, on the other it has justified a godless egoism, vitalism, vulgar will to power and success. It has drawn mankind together and given it a new hope and at the same time crushed it with the burden of a monstrous commercialism."[19]

"There are many conditions and tendencies in human life at present [i.e. after the end of the First World War] which are favourable to the progress of the internationalist idea. The strongest of these favourable forces is the constant drawing closer of the knots of international life, the multiplication of points of contact and threads of communication and an increasing community in thought, in science and knowledge. Science especially has been a great force in its direction; for science is a thing common to all men in its conclusions, open to all in its methods, available to all in its results: it is international in its very nature; there can be no such thing as a national science, but only the nations' contributions to the work and growth of science which are the indivisible inheritance of all humanity. Therefore it is easier for men of science or those strongly influenced by science to grow into the international spirit and the entire world is now beginning to feel the scientific influence and to live in it.

"Science also has created that closer contact of every part of the world with every other part, out of which some sort of international mind is growing. Even cosmopolitan habits of life are now not uncommon and there are a fair number of persons who are as much or more citizens of the world as citizens of their

---

19. Sri Aurobindo: *The Human Cycle,* p. 120.

## 5. Science, Scientism, Modern Technology

own nation. The growth of knowledge is interesting the peoples in each other's art, culture, religion, ideas and is breaking down at many points the prejudice, arrogance and exclusiveness of the old nationalistic sentiment. Religion, which ought to have led the way, but owing to its greater dependence on its external parts and its infrarational rather than its spiritual impulses, has been as much, or even more, a sower of discord as a teacher of unity, – religion is beginning to realise, a little dimly and ineffectively as yet, that spirituality is after all its own chief business and true aim and that it is also the common element and the common bond of all religions."[20]

The second accomplishment of science is that; by its technological realisations which have become the normal environment of humanity at the present time, *it is building a transitional world* between the human being of the bygone civilisations and the new species in the making. This extremely important role of science, seen in the perspective of Sri Aurobindo and the Mother, has not yet been generally perceived.

Thanks to science every person living at present is developing a kind of global consciousness, whether he wants it or not. Television and radio put him in direct contact with his fellow beings everywhere. Telegraph, telephone, fax and the Internet allow him to communicate with his antipodes. He can cover short distances in motorised vehicles and long distances in airplanes. Events in one place of the globe have a direct impact on the life in another place, be it nearby or far-off. Film and television allow for an expanded experience never known before. Electric power turns darkness into daylight and loosens him from the otherwise inescapable rhythm of day and night.

These may seem platitudes, but they acquire a striking significance if one recalls some of the characteristics of the supramental being as described by the Mother e.g. in her talks at the Playground and in a series of encounters with a young disciple, Mona Sarkar, as reported by him in two slim volumes which he has called *Sweet Mother* I and II. The gross physical

---

20. Id., p. 551.

body is heavy, extremely limited in its possibilities, vulnerable, deficient in its perceptions, bound to its age, subject to illness and death, and not unjustly felt by some as a prison. The supramental body will be a body of light, with lightness as one of its characteristics, being able to go where it wishes in an instant and to be at two or more places simultaneously. It will have a supramental, i.e. divine consciousness, even more powerful than the cosmic consciousness; it will contain everything into itself and be present in all things ... True, there is no comparing the capacities of the supramental being with those put at our disposal by the advanced technology of our day. But the portent of the latter becomes very clear if we compare the physical capacities and the horizon of awareness of "ancient man" with those of the supramental being: then the fact that we, at present, live in a kind of intermediate world between what man has been for millennia and the supramental being becomes obvious. The difference between the supramental being and the human being at the very beginning of the Third Millennium is enormous, even unimaginable. Nonetheless, it definitely looks as if our technological wonderworld has its share in preparing the species for a quantum leap that otherwise might be impossible.

Science and materialism have had a third important function, already indicated more than once in this and the previous chapters: to direct man's attention to *Matter* and to increase his knowledge of Matter, which is his "footing". Matter is the direct object of the supramental transformation. Reason, science and commercialisation have now focussed humanity on Matter to a degree unknown at any time in the history of humanity. Sri Aurobindo and the Mother were of course aware of the blatant spiritual shortcomings of a materialistic humanity, but they also appreciated its merits – no doubt because Matter is the level where the supramental transformation has to take place, and is taking place.

## The Future Science

*There is the pressure on human life of an Infinite which will not allow it to rest too long in any formulation.*[21]

– Sri Aurobindo

Materialism, tied up in its circular reasoning that there is only matter because there cannot be anything but matter, has to fade away because of the deficiencies inherent in it as a thought system and as a scientific tool. The Great Chain of Being, in other words the knowledge of the gradations of the manifestation, so obvious to an unprejudiced observer, has been the foundation of all profound thinking; more important, it has been the foundation of all spiritual realisation and knowledge. "Neither the laws nor the possibilities of physical Nature can be entirely known unless we know also the laws and possibilities of supraphysical Nature; therefore the development of new and the recovery of old mental and psychic sciences have to follow upon the perfection of our physical knowledge, and that new era is already beginning to open upon us."[22]

"Science has overpassed itself", wrote Sri Aurobindo already at the beginning of the 20th century, "and must before long be overtaken by a mounting flood of psychological and psychic knowledge which cannot fail to compel quite a new view of the human being and open a new vista before mankind. At the same time the Age of Reason is visibly drawing to an end ..."[23] – "The human mind is beginning to perceive that it has left the heart of almost every problem untouched and illumined only outsides and a certain range of processes. There has been a great and ordered classification and mechanisation, a great discovery and practical result of increasing knowledge, but only on the physical surface of things. Vast abysses of Truth lie below in which are concealed the real springs, the mysterious powers and

---

21. Sri Aurobindo: *The Human Cycle*, p. 168.
22. Id., p. 78.
23. Id., p. 23.

secretly decisive influences of existence. It is a question whether the intellectual reason will ever be able to give us an adequate account of these deeper and greater things or subject them to the intelligent will as it has succeeded in explaining and canalising, though still imperfectly, yet with much show of triumphant result, the forces of physical Nature ... In this limited use of the reason subjected to the rule of an immediate, an apparent vital and physical practicality man cannot rest long satisfied. For his nature pushes him towards the heights; it demands a constant effort of self-transcendence and the impulsion towards things unachieved and even immediately impossible."[24]

"All insistence on the sole or the fundamental validity of the objective real takes its stand on the sense of the basic reality of Matter. But it is now evident that Matter is by no means fundamentally real; it is a structure of Energy: it is becoming even a little doubtful whether the acts and creations of this Energy itself are explicable except as the motions of power of a secret Mind of Consciousness of which its processes and steps of structure are the formulas. It is therefore no longer possible to take Matter as the sole reality. The material interpretation of existence was the result of an exclusive concentration, a preoccupation with one movement of Existence, and such an exclusive concentration has its utility and is therefore permissible; in recent times it has justified itself by the many immense and the innumerable minute discoveries of physical Science. But a solution of the whole problem of existence cannot be based on an exclusive one-sided knowledge; we must know not only what Matter is and what are its processes, but what mind and life are and what are their processes, and one must know also spirit and soul and all that is behind the material surface: only then can we have a knowledge sufficiently integral for a solution of the problem." (*The Life Divine*, pp. 652-53)

"Science is in its own way an occultism", writes Sri Aurobindo, "for it brings to light the formulas which Nature has hidden and it uses its knowledge to set free operations of her energies

---

24. Id., pp. 110-11.

## 5. Science, Scientism, Modern Technology

which she has not included in her ordinary operations and to organise and place at the service of man her occult powers and processes, a vast system of physical magic, – for there is and can be no other magic than the utilisation of secret truths of being, secret powers and processes of Nature. It may even be found that a supraphysical knowledge is necessary for the completion of physical knowledge, because the processes of physical Nature have behind them a supraphysical factor, a power and action mental, vital or spiritual which is not tangible to any outer means of knowledge."[25] Compare this with what Huston Smith writes in his book *Forgotten Truth:* "Ninety per cent of the scientist's universe (some say ninety-nine per cent) is at present invisible; no instruments pick it up, but calculations require that it be posited to account for the gravitational pull on the rims of galaxies. Instruments may yet be invented that will bring this 'dark matter' to light, but even if they are, we will still be left with the wave packets from which particles derive. No scientist expects that those packets will ever be observed. So science is conceding that invisibles exist, and more. It also concedes that these invisibles precede the visible and create or in some way give rise to it."[26]

"Since its very soul is the search for Knowledge, [science] will be unable to cry a halt", Sri Aurobindo predicted. "As it reaches the barriers of sense-knowledge and of the reasoning from sense-knowledge, its very rush will carry it beyond and the rapidity and sureness with which it has embraced the visible universe is only an earnest of the energy and success which we may hope to see repeated in the conquest of what lies beyond, once the stride is taken that crosses the barrier. We see already that advance in its obscure beginnings."[27] [written ca. 1920]

Yes, there may be interesting times ahead.

In 1958, a student of the Ashram school asked the Mother: "Mother, can physical science by its progress open to occultism?" The Mother answered: "It does not call it 'occultism', that

---

25. Sri Aurobindo: *The Life Divine*, p. 652.
26. Huston Smith: *Forgotten Truth*, p. viii.
27. Sri Aurobindo: *The Life Divine*, p. 13.

is all. It's only a matter of words. They are making sensational discoveries – which people with occult knowledge already knew thousands of years ago. They have taken a big detour and are now arriving at the same thing ... They will end up practising occultism without knowing that they are doing so. For, in fact, as soon as one draws close, however slightly, to the truth of things, and when one is sincere in one's search, when one does not remain satisfied by mere appearances, when one really wants to find something and goes deep, deep behind the appearances, then one begins to advance towards the truth of things. And as one comes closer to it, well, one rediscovers the knowledge that others, who began by going within, brought back from their inner discoveries. It's only the method and the path that are different, but the thing discovered will be the same, because there are not two things to be found, there is only one. It will necessarily be the same ... But how hard [the scientists] have been working! [Their work] is, moreover, very respectable."[28]

"There things will remain from the labour of the secularist centuries", wrote Sri Aurobindo, "truth of the physical world and its importance, the scientific method of knowledge, – which is to induce Nature and Being to reveal their own way of being and proceeding, not hastening to put upon them our own impositions of idea and imagination, – and last, though very far from least, the truth and importance of the earth life and the human endeavour, its evolutionary meaning. They will remain, but will turn to another sense and disclose greater issues. Surer of our hope and our labour, we shall see them all transformed into light of a vaster and more intimate world-knowledge and self-knowledge."[29]

---

28. The Mother: *Questions and Answers 1957-58*, pp. 447-48.
29. Sri Aurobindo: *Essays in Philosophy and Yoga*, p. 195.

## 5. Science, Scientism, Modern Technology

## Grumbling humanity

> ... *the quite imaginary perfection of the ideal past* ...[30]
>
> – Sri Aurobindo

> *The crux of the matter is that we are living in a world which we create ourselves, and that we depend on its shortcomings instead of depending on its qualities.*[31]
>
> – Andrei Tarkovsky

Reading the commentators on the present times – philosophers, academic luminaries, journalists, columnists, opinion makers of all kinds, religious leaders ... – is like wading through a swamp of discontent. This is an era of transition, indeed very much so. But how come that the present world is interpreted so negatively by the people living in it? Have considerable parts of humanity ever had it better? Are the glasses of "those whose temperament and imagination dally lovingly with an ideal past"[32] not too rosy-coloured because of a lack of perspective and an insufficient knowledge of the past resulting in an idealisation of it?

"Actually, people are never happy ... The reason probably is that Western man never has known how to live in the present", writes Michel Winock. "All of us are living with the opinion that the past was better. In most cases this is nothing but an illusion. As nowadays we can interrogate with some precision the main currents of public opinion, we can measure the load of dissatisfaction weighing on the people, even when they become richer, live to a greater age, and acquire an amelioration of their living conditions their grandparents could not have dreamed of. For nothing is more difficult than to live in the present tense: the past tense and, better still, the conditional tense save us from the worries and uncertainties of everyday life. Nothing is

---

30. Sri Aurobindo: *The Human Cycle*, 198.
31. Andrei Tarkovsky, quoted in the magazine *Nouvelles Clés*.
32. Sri Aurobindo: *Essays in Philosophy and Yoga*, p. 184.

more dreadful than to live in the instability of days following one after the other, the near future always remaining insecure. The very same persons who, when interviewed in the past about their existence, denied its advantages, imagine today that same past as lost happiness. Yesterday is always better than today. Nostalgia is a malady of the senile."[33] – "The sigh of the extreme conservative mind for the golden age of the past, which was not so golden as it appears to an imaginative eye in the distance", writes Sri Aurobindo, "is a vain breath blown to the winds by the rush of the car of the Time-Spirit in the extreme velocity of its progress."[34]

"I find this contemporary cult of pessimism scandalous", writes Christiane Collange, a French journalist, in her *Merci, mon siècle* (Thank you, my century), in which she thanks the 20th century for all the marvels and ameliorations it has brought into so many lives. She fully agrees with Michel Winock: "Happiness does not have a very good reputation with us; optimism is accused of irresponsibility; enjoyment, small or big, does not yet occupy the place it deserves to have; satisfaction in its various forms hardly dares to be experienced and to show itself in broad daylight. On the contrary suffering, difficulty and bad luck give right to social consideration; sacrifice and austerity are still considered to be exemplary; pessimism is widely publicised."[35]

Just one example of the current evaluation of one of the wonders of the present world: television. "Television alienates the mind, shows everyone the same, transmits the ideology of those who produce it, corrupts the imagination of the children, reduces the curiosity of the adults, puts the thinking mind to sleep, is an instrument of political control, dictates the way in which we think, manipulates the information, imposes dominant cultural models (not to say bourgeois models), shows systematically only one part of reality omitting the urban classes, the middle classes, the tertiary classes, life in the countryside, the world of the labourer, marginalizes the regional languages

---

33. Martin Winock: *Chronique des années soixante*, pp. 115 and 265-66.
34. Sri Aurobindo: *The Human Cycle*, p. 488.
35. Christiane Collange: *Merci, mon siècle*, p. 159.

## 5. Science, Scientism, Modern Technology

and cultures, causes passivity, destroys the interpersonal relations within the family, eradicates the reading habit and all 'difficult' forms of culture, incites to violence, to vulgarity and pornography, prevents the children from becoming adults", etc., for a whole page more. This sorry litany has been assembled from statements in diverse publications by the French philosopher Luc Ferry and published in his book *L'Homme-Dieu*.[36] Similar litanies could be made about the radio, the computer, the telephone, the automobile, the airplane, and the cinema.

It might therefore be interesting to give one or two examples of how things were in times gone by. We will not choose what would now be considered the "inhuman" instance of the "care" for the babies as practised let us say less than two centuries ago, a time when child mortality was a fact of everyday life, and also documented in the same book by Ferry. Or the medieval relation between husband and wife, which according to contemporary standards should be one of mutual appreciation if not love. Or the way the victorious party in whatever kind of past war was generally supposed to behave towards the defeated. Or the way household personnel and workers, not to speak of the serfs, were treated. Some well-documented history lessons on these subjects might give the earthlings of the present day a more realistic understanding of life in the past and of the dissimilarity with their own normal, contemporary, "human" world.

We choose, firstly, a brief evocation of life in Elizabethan London. "Most Elizabethans have bad breath, rotting teeth, constant stomach disorders, and scabs or running sores all over their skin. Things are no better on a public scale. The city ditches are used as toilets. Butchers throw dead animal carcasses into the street to rot. Housewives nonchalantly toss putrid garbage into the river [Thames]. Poor people are buried in mass graves, and the bodies of the rich, lying beneath the church building in burial vaults, force the congregation to evacuate

---

36. Luc Ferry: *L'Homme-Dieu*, p. 136 (footnote).

because the stench of the decomposition is too strong ..."[37] Our second example is a description of the river Seine in Paris as recently as 1880: "The banks of the Seine presented us with a sad view: the river, full with waste of all kinds (vegetables, hair, animal carcasses, etc.), was really abhorrent; a grey slime, in which that organic refuse got stuck, accumulated all along the border; it caused an active fermentation resulting in gas bubbles of an often considerable dimension."[38]

That pessimism is ingrained in man is understandable if we consider his nature. He incarnates in body after body at a stage of evolution that still is completely problematical, in a time of transition when most of his physical and psychological composition still is predominantly animal-like. The dominant level of his nature – and this is still very little understood – is his subconscious, so much so that it may be said that the conscious part of his personality is not much more than a few leaves floating on a mud pool. It is the subconscious that determinates his vital being, full of fright, insecurity, egoism, aggression, cruelty. And it is his vital being that predominantly determines his mentalisations and thinking. Add to that a physical body subject to injury, illness and death, subject to a sexual urge that may be unsubduable, confused and insecure, and a life in the company of beings in the same tangled situation – and one has more than sufficient reason for a sort of ineradicable constitutional pessimism. Sri Aurobindo wrote that this *condition humaine* (human condition) was susceptible to the "downward gravitation", the easy giving in to the burden and even evil of life, contrary to the upward movement of any idealistic human endeavour and the spiritual effort.

Another factor contributing to the pessimism and negative evaluation of the present period is that the appreciation of its values is in most cases the opinion of the mass, of average man. In our time "elitism" is a dirty word. It is an assumption of postmodernism that "high" and "low" have to be mingled,

---

37. Joseph Papp and Elizabeth Kirkland: *Shakespeare alive!*, p. 10.
38. Christiane Collange: *Merci, mon siècle*, p. 170.

## 5. Science, Scientism, Modern Technology

and therefore that mass culture is what suits our era. It is rather astonishing that many of the cleverest heads of our time, mostly French proponents of what is known as "structuralism", found pleasure, authority and power in contending that the individual, the subject, is dead. Often quoted words in this context are the very last phrase of Michel Foucault's *The Order of Things:* "[If the thesis of this book is correct] then one can certainly wager that man will be erased, like a face drawn in sand at the edge of the sea."[39]

Structuralism, like all important philosophical movements, was based on a kernel of truth, but, like all important philosophical movements, a truth deformed by its exaggeration and exclusiveness. "By individual we mean normally something that separates itself from everything else and stands apart, though in reality there is no such thing anywhere in existence; it is a figment of our mental conceptions useful and necessary to express a partial and practical truth", writes Sri Aurobindo. But he adds: "It is necessary to insist, that by the true individual we mean nothing of the kind but a conscious power of being of the Eternal, always existing by unity, always capable of mutuality. It is that being which by self-knowledge enjoys liberation and immortality."[40] Alas – and here we touch again upon the fundamental flaw in the Western world view and the vain groping of its thought for truth, reality, reliable fundamentals – the essential structure of the human being and the manifestation it is part of remain unrecognised, and therefore constitute the enormous underwater part of the iceberg while Western thought and comprehension dance, more and more in desperation, on the surface of its visible top.

In contrast to the above, thus forming one of the many apparent contradictions in this transitional time, is the fact that humanity enjoys at present, especially in the West, one of the high seasons, if not the highest ever, of individualism. "There is no doubt that the right to be absolutely oneself, to

---
39. Michel Foucault: *The Order of Things: An Archaeology of the Human Sciences,* p. 387.
40. Sri Aurobindo: *The Life Divine,* p. 373.

enjoy life at its fullest, is inseparable from a society that has posited the free individual as a cardinal value ... We are experiencing a second individualist revolution ... It is everywhere the search for an own identity and no longer universality that motivates the social and individual actions ... Hedonist and personalist individualism has become lawful and does not meet with opposition any longer ... This is a personalised society where the important thing is to be oneself ... The postmodern culture is a vector for the widening of individualism ..." All these quotations are from a widely influential book by Gilles Lipovetsky *L'Ère du vide - Essais sur l'individualisme contemporain* (The Era of Emptiness: Essays on contemporary individualism) first published in 1983.[41]

The individual, however, seems scarcely capable of bearing the freedom it has gained and which is, as we have seen in a previous chapter, the chief realisation of the Western effort. Isn't it amazing that everything man has been dreaming of throughout all of history becomes problematic once he gets it – for example unheard of material possibilities and individual freedom to a high degree? "No political ideology is able to fire the masses any longer. Postmodern society has no more idols or taboos, no glorious image of itself, no animating historical project. Henceforward we are dominated by emptiness,"[42] writes Lipovetsky. An explanation may be that material well-being as such is no fulfilment of the needs and the growth of the soul, and that full individuality can be realised only when the human being will be recognised for what it is, in all its aspects. This should be kept in mind when reflecting on the generalised malaise humanity is subject to at a time that, materially, people never had it so good.

"Peace we do not have, but we do have abundance!" says the Frenchman Jacques Lacarrière. "I often maintain that in a supermarket of today one can find the near-totality of what the human being has dreamt to have since the time he was

---

41. Gilles Lipovetsky: *L'Ère du vide*, passim.
42. Id., p. 16.

## 5. Science, Scientism, Modern Technology

living in caves."[43] We listen once more to the British historian Eric Hobsbawm: "Let us not forget that, measured by whatever standard, the majority of the individuals live better at the end of the 20th century, this in spite of the terrible catastrophes that occurred in it ... After all, India has not known a famine since 1943. Apart from a few rare exceptions, the human beings no longer have to live with hunger in the major part of the world. This means that, for the very first time, the production is up to the demand of the mass of the population. In the developed countries people live no longer in the age of the elementary necessities and can choose what they want instead of having to choose between having nothing to eat and not having a roof over their head. They do not have to worry anymore about their daily bread, except in order to decide whether they prefer a sandwich or a toast with cooked or smoked ham on a bed of fresh or dry tomatoes ... The productive growth and the availability of the riches are enormous, and the majority of the world population has benefited from them. This is a characteristic of the 20th century that has to be taken into consideration when one evaluates the good and bad aspects of an era ..."[44]

Christiane Collange, with the practical eye of a journalist, a housewife and a grandmother of twelve, thanks the 20th century for the following reasons: the improvements in the field of health; the lessening of the burden of daily life; the liberalisation of the human relations; the revolutions in the field of communications; the improvements in transportation; the heightening of personal well-being; the better opportunities for children; the widening of the cultural availabilities; and the choices women have acquired. It is an impressive list – still more impressive when compared to the lives of our ancestors.

"In contrast to the picture propagated by certain media", she writes optimistically, "materialism, violence and hatred are not omnipresent in our society; on the contrary, the indications of the 'new age' are everywhere and signal an intense need to

---

43. In: *La grande Mutation – Enquête sur la fin d'un millénaire*, p. 143.
44. In: *Les Enjeux du XXIe siècle – Entretien avec Antonio Polito*, pp. 97-98.

find meaning again, to develop affective ties of a better quality, rather than to wallow in consumption or to immure oneself within a hardened egocentrism. All the observers of our mentalities discern this new tendency towards a higher human value."[45]

She is not the only one to report positive signs. Even Gilles Lipovetsky writes: "The crisis of the modern societies is in the first place cultural or spiritual"; and: "Simultaneously with the revolution of the information science, the postmodern societies experience an 'inner revolution', an immense 'change of consciousness' ('awareness movement'), an unprecedented dedication to the knowledge and accomplishment of oneself as demonstrated by the proliferation of psy-groups, techniques of expression and communication, meditation and oriental gymnastics."[46] Often quoted are the words of André Malraux: "The 21st century will be spiritual or it will not be."

Putting everything together, it becomes clear that any negative interpretation of the facts of our present world can be countered with a positive interpretation of the very same facts, as shown in the enumeration of the topics in Collange's book.[47] This positive interpretation is possible because we are living in a time of transition when a certain past is dying and a certain future is being born. The change on all levels of life is so bewildering because the transition is a tremendous one, from the human being to the supramental, divine being. Not only can the period in which we live be called "postmodern"; it can also, and with better justification, be called "presupramental". It bears repetition that the vision of Sri Aurobindo and the Mother is the only one applicable to times like these, because their vision did not originate from human shortsightedness, however philosophical, but from a suprarational avataric knowledge and

---

45. Catherine Collange: op. cit., p. 97.
46. Gilles Lipovetsky: op. cit., pp. 122 and 76.
47. "Most things that the human mind thus alternately trumpets and bans are a double skein. They come to us with opposite faces, their good side and their bad, a dark aspect of error and a bright of truth; and it is as we look upon one or the other visage that we swing to our extremes of opinion or else oscillate between them." (Sri Aurobindo: *Essays in Philosophy and Yoga*, p. 185).

## 5. Science, Scientism, Modern Technology

intention. Whether the world knows it or not, a Force is acting and will not be countermanded.

Between the descent of the rational mind and the first human beings about one million years elapsed, according to the Mother. Now that the Supermind has descended things will go faster. She and Sri Aurobindo estimated that it would be three hundred years before the visible, concrete appearance of the first supramental being. But in the meantime Overman and Overwoman are taking the lead in the march of humanity, and what is necessary to happen will be worked out through them, unseen.

# 6

# The Supramental "Catastrophe"

> ... *the anarchy of our being which covers our confused attempt at a new order* ...[1]
>
> – Sri Aurobindo

> *Suddenly, there is a curve in the road, a turning point. Somewhere, the real scene has been lost, the scene where you had rules for the game and some solid stakes that everybody could rely on.*[2]
>
> – Jean Baudrillard

In 1972 the Mother said: "For centuries and centuries humanity has waited for this time. It has come. But it's difficult. I don't simply tell you we are here upon earth to rest and enjoy ourselves, now is not the time for that. We are here to prepare the way for the new creation.

"The body [her body] has some difficulty, so I can't be active, alas. It's not because I am old: I am not old. I am not old, I am younger than most of you. If I am here inactive, it's because the body has given itself definitely to prepare the transformation. But the consciousness is clear and we are here to work. Rest and enjoyment will come afterwards. Let's do our work here. So I've called you to tell you that. Take what you can, do what you can, my help will be with you. All sincere effort will be helped to the maximum."[3]

"It's the hour to be heroic. Heroism is not what it's usually

---

1. Sri Aurobindo: *The Human Cycle*, p. 127.
2. Quoted in Steven Best and Douglas Kellner: *The Postmodern Turn*, p. 4.
3. This was spoken in English; from here she went on in French.

## 6. The Supramental "Catastrophe"

said to be: it is to become wholly unified.[4] And the divine help will always be with those who have resolved to be heroic in full sincerity. That's what I have to say."

"You are here at this moment – that's to say upon earth – because you have chosen so in the past.[5] (You don't remember that any more, but I do.) That is why you are here. Well, you must rise to the height of the task. You must do your utmost, you must conquer all pettiness and limitations. Above all you must say to your ego: 'Your time is past.' We want a race without ego, that has a divine Consciousness in place of the ego. *That* is what we want: the divine Consciousness that will allow the race to develop and the supramental being to be born."[6]

Like every kind of birth in our universe the birth of a new era in the development of the manifestation is a dramatic event, invisibly prepared and in its consequences unforeseeable. The pain of a mother's labour cannot be expressed in words. It is that cosmic moment when two lives are at stake and Destiny holds both in its hand. Likewise, when a new era is born "the confusion becomes all the more intense and dark at the time the light is about to dawn."[7]

"The better things that are to come are preparing or growing under a veil and the worse are prominent everywhere,"[8] wrote Sri Aurobindo in 1946 (i.e. ten years before the manifestation of the Supermind). In 1947 he wrote: "I myself foresaw that this worst would come, the darkness of night before the dawn; therefore I am not discouraged. I know what is preparing behind the darkness and can see and feel the first signs of its coming."[9] And in 1948: "I am afraid I can hold but cold comfort – for the present at least – to those of your correspondents who are lamenting the present state of things. Things are bad, are grow-

---

4. By this the Mother means that all parts of the being should be unified around the central being in man: the psychic being. Only then is man fully master of himself – the conquest that demands the greatest heroism.
5. I.e. in one of the past incarnations.
6. The Mother: *Notes on the Way*, p. 307.
7. Id., p. 175.
8. Sri Aurobindo: *On Himself*, p. 168.
9. Id., p. 171.

ing worse and may at any time grow worst or worse than worst if that is possible – and anything however paradoxical seems possible in the present perturbed world. The best thing for them [the correspondents in question] is to realise that all this was necessary because certain possibilities had to emerge and be got rid of, if a new and better world was at all to come into being; it would not have done to postpone them for a later time[10] ... But they must remember too that the new world whose coming we envisage is not to be made of the same texture as the old and different only in pattern, and that it must come by other means – from within and not from without; so the best way is not to be too much preoccupied with the lamentable things that are happening outside, but themselves to grow within so that they may be ready for the new world, whatever form it may take."[11]

"At the present stage", wrote Sri Aurobindo in 1947, "the progressive supramentalisation of the Overmind is the first immediate preoccupation and a second is the lightening of the heavy resistance of the Inconscient."[12] He will in the end have to descend, in 1950, into death voluntarily in order to tackle the problem at the root of things in Death's own den. Six years later, in 1956, the supramental Consciousness established itself in the earth-atmosphere. The turning point was reached, and the historians lost their bearings to further interpret what was happening on the planet. Said Sri Aurobindo: "I have never had a strong and persistent will for anything to happen in the world – I am not speaking of personal things – which did not eventually happen even after delay, defeat or even disaster."[13]

The Mother knew what was going on because she saw it, was involved in it and even caused it. That is why she spoke of "the supramental catastrophe" the world was undergoing: this "catastrophe" was the inevitable process of the most momentous

---

10. Sri Aurobindo alludes here, among other things, to the Second World War, in which the Asura who possessed Hitler had to be defeated. See the chapters on the Second World War in Georges Van Vrekhem's *Beyond Man* and *The Mother* (HarperCollins India).
11. Sri Aurobindo: *On Himself,* pp. 171-72.
12. Id., p. 170.
13. Id., p. 169.

## 6. The Supramental "Catastrophe"

change not only in the history of humanity but in the course of evolution on this Earth. Things were no longer as they had been, she said in the last years of her embodiment. "This really is a new world." "There is something like a golden Force, without material consistence and yet apparently enormously heavy, that is pressing down upon Matter in order to compel it to turn towards the Divine *inwardly* – not an outward escape *(gesture upward)* – to turn towards the Divine *inwardly*. Because of this the apparent result is as if catastrophes were inevitable. But along with this perception of inevitable catastrophes there are solutions to the situation, events that seem to be utterly miraculous. It is as if the two extremes were becoming more extreme, as if what is good were becoming better and what is bad were becoming worse. That's how it is – with that formidable Power *pressing* – upon the world."[14] The result of the supramental transformation was certain and would come about with a minimum of damage, but that minimum, according to the Mother, might still be considerable.

"[Great catastrophic upheavals after the descent of the Supermind] there need not be", wrote Sri Aurobindo reassuring a disciple. "There will necessarily be great changes but they are not bound to be catastrophic. When there is a strong pressure from overmind forces for change, then there are likely to be catastrophes because of the resistance and clash of forces. The supramental has a greater – in its fullness a complete – mastery of things and power of harmonisation which can overcome resistance by other means than dramatic struggle and violence."[15]

"The future of the earth depends on a change of consciousness", wrote the Mother in a message of 1964. "The only hope for the future is a change of man's consciousness and the change is bound to come. But it is left to men to decide if they will collaborate for this change or if it will have to be enforced upon them by the power of crushing circumstances."[16] She also said: "Nothing but a radical change of consciousness can save

---

14. The Mother: *Notes on the Way*, p. 313 (emphasis in the text).
15. Sri Aurobindo: *Letters on Yoga*, p. 33.
16. *Words of the Mother*, CWM 15, p. 66.

humanity from the terrible plight into which it is plunged." And again: "A new world, based on Truth and refusing the old slavery to falsehood, wants to take birth. In all countries there are people who know it, at least feel it. To them we call: 'Will you collaborate?'"[17]

In the last quotation from Sri Aurobindo, he makes a distinction between the action of the Overmind, which is the world of the Gods, and the action of the Supermind. The Supermind, being a Consciousness of Unity and Harmony, acts in the manifestation as a whole, harmoniously and inescapably, with its divine omnipotence. This is the reason why Sri Aurobindo and the Mother worked unceasingly and one-pointedly for its descent into the earth-atmosphere and were never satisfied with partial realisation. This fundamental rationale of their whole avataric effort has been very little understood and is generally interpreted within the context of traditional spirituality, while it was something completely different. The Gods are cosmic forces, each of them representing the One; from this results that their action can only be partial – Overmind is situated on the "fault" in the universal manifestation where the One becomes the many – and that the consequences of their action are always fragmentary and often result in clashes among themselves and with their titanic adversaries. This is what the greatest part of all mythologies in the world is about.

Having explained this, Sri Aurobindo warns against another possible misunderstanding. "A mental control can only be a control, not a cure; a mental teaching, rule, standard, can only impose an artificial groove in which our action revolves mechanically or with difficulty and which imposes a curbed and limited formation on the course of our nature. A total change of consciousness, a radical change of nature is the one remedy and the sole issue."[18] As he wrote to Nirodbaran, all efforts of the mind and the overmind can yield nothing but partial results. "The absoluteness can only come with a supra-

---

17. Id., p. 67.
18. Sri Aurobindo: *The Life Divine*, p. 628.

## 6. The Supramental "Catastrophe"

mental change. For below the supramental it is an action of a Force among many forces – in the supramental it becomes a law of the nature."[19] Nature is being made anew. "Evolution itself is evolving."

The problem, however, is that the substance of Supermind is so different from the kind of substance we are made of and are used to. Beings like us can live in gross matter, on a planet consisting of gross matter, but to live in the Supermind means no less than to live in the Sun, metaphorically speaking. This explains the necessity of a period of transition and of transitional beings which the Mother called "overman". When she went through the process of transformation in her body, she said more than once that its temperature became so hot that she thought it would burst, and she thanked "the Lord" for the care with which he dosed the progress of the transformation, adapting it to her body's capacities. The supramental substance "is not the substance we know at present", she said, and if the Supermind in its full power appeared suddenly on the earth "everybody would disappear."[20] – "Sri Aurobindo has said ... that if the divine Consciousness, the divine Power, the divine Love, the Truth, manifested too rapidly upon the earth, the earth would be dissolved! She would not be able to stand it!"[21]

### The Family of the Aspiration

"You are on the earth at this moment because you have chosen so in the past", said the Mother to her youthful audience at the Ashram Playground. "If you go deep enough where all outer things are as silent as can be, you will find within that flame of which I often speak, and in that flame you will see your destiny. You will see a centuries-old aspiration that has

---

19. Nirodbaran: *Correspondence with Sri Aurobindo*, p. 191.
20. The Mother: *Notes on the Way*, pp. 56 ff.
21. Id., p. 85.

concentrated little by little to lead you through countless births to the great day of the realisation – a preparation which has been made in the course of thousands of years and will now reach its culmination."[22]

"Some psychic beings have come here [in the Ashram] who are ready to join with great lines of consciousness above, represented often by beings of the higher planes, and are therefore specially fitted to join with the Mother intimately in the great work that has to be done. These have all [a] special relation with the Mother which adds to the past one,"[23] wrote Sri Aurobindo. "Some have come with her to share in the work, others she had called, others have come seeking for the light."[24] They were "the souls destined to the way of the integral yoga," "the rare souls that were ripe," "the pioneer few."

The Mother's first question when she met Aurobindo Ghose for the first time, in 1914, had been: "Should you do your yoga, attain the goal, and then afterwards take up the work with others, or should you immediately let all those who have the same aspiration gather around you and go forward all together towards the goal? Because of my earlier work and all that I had tried out", said the Mother many years later, "I came to Sri Aurobindo with this question very precisely formulated. For the two possibilities were there: either to practise an intensive individual *sadhana* by withdrawing from the world, that is, by no longer having any contact with others, or to let the group be formed naturally and spontaneously, not preventing it from being formed, allowing it to form by itself, and starting all together on the path. Well, the decision was not at all a mental choice, it came spontaneously. The circumstances were such that no choice was required. I mean, quite naturally, spontaneously, the group was formed in such a way that it became an imperious necessity. And so, once you have started like that, it is settled, you have to go on like that to the end."[25]

---

22. The Mother: *Questions and Answers 1954,* pp. 271-2.
23. Sri Aurobindo: *On the Mother,* p. 168.
24. Id., p. 170.
25. The Mother: *Questions and Answers 1955,* p. 414.

## 6. The Supramental "Catastrophe"

"How come that we have met?" an English lady once asked the Mother. The Mother answered: "We have all been together in former lives, otherwise we would not have been able to meet in this life. All of us belong to the same family, and we have worked together through the centuries for the victory of the Divine and His manifestation upon the earth."[26] – "If you have in you the sincere aspiration to find those who, like you, are in search of something, you will always be put in a position to meet them in one way or another, in totally unexpected circumstances."[27] – "It is ages of ardent aspiration that have brought us here to do the Divine's Work."[28]

"When people, who are born dispersed over the world at great distances from one another, are driven by circumstances or by an inner impulsion to come together here, it is almost always because they have met in some previous life (not all in the same life), and because their psychic being felt that they belong to the same family. So they have taken an inner vow to continue to act together and to collaborate. This is why, even though they are born far from one another, there is 'something' that compels them to come and get together. [This 'something'] is the psychic being, the psychic consciousness behind. And it is only to the extent that the psychic consciousness is strong enough to arrange, to organise the external circumstances or the life, that it is strong enough, that is, not to be counteracted by outside forces, by the external events of life, that one can meet."

"This is profoundly true in reality [i.e. in the material world]. There are large 'families of beings' who work for the same cause, who have gathered in more or less large numbers and who come [down upon earth] in groups, as it were. It is as if at certain times there were awakenings in the psychic world, as if lots of sleeping children were being woken up: 'It's time! Quick, quick, you have to go down [to the earth]!' and they hurry down. And sometimes they do not touch down at the same place, they are dispersed. But there is something within that causes

---
26. The Mother: *Questions and Answers 1929*, p. 5.
27. The Mother: *Questions and Answers 1950-51*, p. 287.
28. *Words of the Mother*, CWM 13, p. 112.

an uneasiness, that pushes them on. For some reason they feel attracted [to a certain place] and that brings them together."[29]

"That is the true family: the family of the aspiration, the family of the spiritual tendency", said the Mother.[30] And to the people who had confided their lives to her she said: "It is ages of ardent aspiration that have brought us here to do the Divine's Work."[31] She called them *les bien-né*: "the well-born", or "the few", "the predestined", "the pioneers", "the avant-garde", "those who have in them a spiritual destiny and are born to realise the Divine". "To follow the path of spiritual experience", she said, "one must have within oneself a 'spiritual being,'[32] one must be 'twice born', as it is said. For if one does not have a spiritual being within which is at least at the point of becoming self-aware, one may try to imitate these [spiritual] experiences, but it will only be a crude imitation or hypocrisy, it will not be real."[33] It is of this "family of the aspiration" whom Sri Aurobindo said: "Throughout the course of history, a small minority has been carrying the torch to save humanity in spite of itself."[34]

The following question was put to Sri Aurobindo: "In her book 'Conversations' [1929] the Mother says: 'We have all met in previous lives … and have worked through the ages for the victory of the Divine.' Is it true of all people who come and stay here [i.e. in the Ashram]? What about so many who came and went away?" Sri Aurobindo answered: "Those who went away are also of these and still are of that circle. Temporary checks do not make any difference to the essential truth of the soul's seeking."[35]

---

29. The Mother: *Questions and Answers 1953*, p. 2. As to what the Mother said about the families of artists who have come down on earth together in order to create the "golden ages": of the great civilisations, see the chapter "Artist among the artists" in *The Mother* by Georges Van Vrekhem.
30. The Mother: *Questions and Answers 1950-51*, p. 259.
31. *Words of the Mother*, CWM 13, p. 112.
32. By "spiritual being" the Mother here means a soul, or divine spark, that in the course of its reincarnations has developed a mature "psychic being".
33. The Mother: *Questions and Answers 1957-58*, pp. 344-45.
34. Nirodbaran: *Talks with Sri Aurobindo* I, p. 241.
35. Sri Aurobindo: *On Himself*, p. 450.

## 6. The Supramental "Catastrophe"

"What Sri Aurobindo promised and what naturally interests us, we who are here now", said the Mother in October 1956, "is that the time has come when some beings among the élite[36] of humanity, who fulfil the conditions necessary for spiritualization, will be able to transform their bodies with the help of the supramental Force, Consciousness and Light, so as no longer to be animal-men but overmen.[37] Sri Aurobindo has made this promise, and he based it on the knowledge he had that the supramental Force was on the point of manifesting on the earth. In fact, it had descended into him long ago; he knew it, and he knew what its effects were. And now that it has manifested universally, generally, I may say [on 29 February 1956], the certitude of the possibility of transformation is of course still greater. There is no longer any doubt that those who will fulfil or who now fulfil the conditions are on the way towards this transformation."[38] Reading the above quotations from the Mother, does one have to conclude that "the family of the aspiration", the souls who have descended to undertake the great but demanding job of the transformation, were or are to be found exclusively at the Sri Aurobindo Ashram, in Pondicherry, South India? In August 1957, one year after the descent of the Supermind, the Mother said the following: "It is only quite recently that the need for a collective reality began to appear, which remains not necessarily limited to the Ashram but embraces all who have declared themselves – I don't mean materially but in their consciousness – to be disciples of Sri Aurobindo, and who have tried to live his teaching. Among all of them, and more pronouncedly since the manifestation of the supramental Consciousness and Force, there has awakened the necessity for a true communal life, which would not be based

---

36. Ken Wilber: "But isn't this view of mine terribly elitist? Good heavens, I hope so. When you go to a basketball game, do you want to see me or Michael Jordan play basketball? ... All excellence is elitist, and that includes spiritual excellence as well." (In the magazine *What is Enlightenment?*, issue 12, p. 28.)
37. The Mother says here in the original French *surhommes*, but again the world has been wrongly translated as "superman" (in the singular).
38. The Mother: *Questions and Answers 1956*, p. 323.

only on purely material circumstances, but which would represent a deeper truth and be the beginning of what Sri Aurobindo calls a supramental or gnostic community.

"He has of course said that, to this end, the individuals constituting this collectivity should themselves have the supramental consciousness. But even without attaining an individual perfection – even while still being very far from it – there was at the same time an inner effort to create this 'collective individuality', so to speak. The need for a real union, a deeper bond has been felt and the effort has been directed towards that realisation ... *The effort which you will be able to make individually, instead of being only an individual progress, will spread, it will have very important collective results.*"[39]

And the Mother said in the same month: "[The global condition] is not very bright. But for us one possibility remains. Even if on the outside things deteriorate completely and a catastrophe cannot be avoided, there remains for us, I mean for those to whom the supramental life is not a vain dream, those who have faith in its reality and the aspiration to realise it – I don't necessarily mean those who are gathered here in Pondicherry, in the Ashram, but *those who have between them the link which the knowledge Sri Aurobindo has given them and the will to live according to this knowledge* – there remains for them the possibility to intensify their aspiration, their will, their effort, to marshal their energies and shorten the time for the realisation."[40]

These words bring to mind a book that caused quite a furore in the 1980s, namely Marilyn Ferguson's *The Aquarian Conspiracy*. The author had no idea of the Supermind, but she had a finely tuned sense of the times. Her central thesis is that people everywhere are looking towards a "shuddering" change and feel united in this expectation. "The social activism of the 1960s and the 'consciousness revolution' of the early 1970s seemed to be moving towards a historic synthesis: social transformation resulting from personal transformation – change from the inside

---

39. The Mother: *Questions and Answers 1957-58*, pp. 172-73 (emphasis added).
40. Id., p. 169 (emphasis added).

## 6. The Supramental "Catastrophe"

out." (p. 18) – "The great shuddering, irrevocable shift overtaking us is not a new political, religious, or philosophical system. It is a new mind – the ascendance of a startling worldview that gathers into its framework breakthrough science and insights from earliest recorded thought." (p. 23) – "A revolution that is just getting under way, like a scientific revolution, is initially dismissed as crazy or unlikely. While it is clearly in progress, it seems alarming and threatening. In retrospect, when power has changed hands, it appears to have been foreordained." (p. 40) – "What the world lives by at the moment just will not do. Nor will it; nor do very many people suppose any longer that it will. Countries like ours are full of people who have all the material comforts they desire, yet lead lives of quiet (and at times noisy) desperation, understanding nothing but the fact that there is a hole inside them and that however much food and drink they pour into it, however many motorcars and television sets they stuff it with, however many well-balanced children and loyal friends they parade around the edges of it ... it aches." (p. 42) The Mother deemed the feeling of that "hole" inside, *ce besoin*, the need for the experience of fullness and integrality, for the unexplainable "something" worth living for, the starting point of the yogic effort leading to the transformation. – "Given what we are learning about the nature of profound change, transformation of the human species seems less and less improbable." (p. 172).

The mature souls, incarnated on earth to help bring about the supramental transformation, are not numerous. On 24 November 1965, a *darshan* day, Sri Aurobindo had been present from morning till night, and he had shown the Mother the state of humanity and its future evolution (which will be described in the next chapter). "... And then there were the few", said the Mother, "the rare individuals who were ready for the necessary effort to prepare the transformation and to draw the new forces, to try to make Matter adapt, to seek the means of expression, etc. These are ready for the yoga of Sri Aurobindo. They are very few in number. There are even those who have the sense of sacrifice and are ready for a hard, difficult life if it would lead or contribute to the future transformation. But they should not, they should not in any way try to influence the others and make them share in their own effort; it would be altogether wrong – not only wrong, but extremely inept, for it would change the universal rhythm and movement, or at least the terrestrial movement, and instead of helping, it would create conflicts and end in chaos ..."

"It was like the vision of a great universal Rhythm in which each thing takes its place and everything is all right. And the effort for transformation, reduced to a small number, becomes a thing much more precious and much more powerful for the realisation. It is as though a choice has been made for those who will be the pioneers of the new creation. And all those ideas of 'spreading', of 'preparing' or 'churning Matter' are childishness. They are human restlessness. The vision was of a beauty so majestic and so calm, so smiling, oh! It was full, truly full of the divine Love. And not a divine Love that 'pardons', it is not like that at all: each thing in its place, realising its inner rhythm as perfectly as possible."[41]

The more the Mother's body became supramentalised, the more its realisations spread in the body of humanity. For a supramentalised cell is no longer an individual in the separate, egoistic sense – the supramental Consciousness and ego do not agree – it is divinely omnipresent, as the supramental body will be omnipresent. Therefore the Mother sometimes quipped that coming into contact with her was contagious. "The power of spiritual contagion", she said, was "the only efficacious one" to communicate one's spiritual realisation. "The only thing that is truly effective is the possibility of transferring to others the state of consciousness in which one lives oneself. But one cannot improvise this power; one cannot imitate it; one cannot do as if one has it ... If one sincerely wants to help the others and the world, the best thing one can do is to be oneself what one wants others to be, not only as an example, but because one becomes

---

41. The Mother: *Notes on the Way*, pp. 24-25.

## 6. The Supramental "Catastrophe"

a centre of radiating power which, by the very fact that it exists, compels the rest of the world to transform itself."[42]

She felt more and more that there were responses everywhere in the world. *Beaucoup de gens,* many people, had extraordinary experiences, caused by the new Force, without knowing it. What happened in her body, the Mother said, had repercussion in all bodies that were receptive, wherever. "I know that there are people everywhere on earth" taken up into the movement of transformation. Ferguson's *Aquarian Conspiracy* is but seldom referred to any more, but it was a much truer premonition than she herself may have thought when writing it two decades ago.

We end this section about "the family of the aspiration" with two notes in the margin. The first one is that the Mother stressed countless times the necessity of heroism, courage and the warrior spirit for the ones who were fighting the battle in the spiritual vanguard of the new age. *"C'est le moment d'être héroïque:* it's the time to be heroic", she said. And Sri Aurobindo had written: "Without heroism man cannot grow into the Godhead."[43] In this era of pacifism, after the protests against the war in Vietnam and like-minded movements, an exhortation to braveness is often looked at askance, but this betrays an ignorance of what spiritual transformation actually means. Most people come to the yoga for quietude and peace, for release from the stressful burden that living in an earthly body means. Their intention is justified and praiseworthy, and the established spiritual paths are meant to provide just that. The Integral Yoga of Sri Aurobindo and the Mother, though, seeks to take evolution a step ahead, which means to transform the present condition of the planet and of humanity. But humanity and the planet are dominated by forces hostile to the Divine, opposed to any kind of transformation, and they will never let go of their supremacy if they are not compelled to. The change in the existing world order depends on the fiat of the Divine, implemented through his embodiment as an Avatar, and worked out through

---

42. The Mother: *Questions and Answers 1957-58,* pp. 416-17.
43. Sri Aurobindo: *The Human Cycle,* p. 166.

the spreading of the new powers established by the Avatar in Matter. The spreading of these powers is the work of the "ripe souls" that have incarnated in order to accomplish this very job. Any spiritual effort is as much as possible thwarted by the hostile forces. These beings exist on all lower levels of existence, as well on what is for us "inside" as on what we experience as "outside". In fact, the ignorant human being is to them what the mouse is to the cat, for everything that to us is occult is their domain. Western man hardly believes in the devil any more, and evil has become a metaphor. Disbelief in the devil is understandable because, as is the case with all things occult, Christianity had presented him in a too ridiculous form. The East has a much more thorough occult knowledge of "the devil", of the anti-divine beings in their various shapes and levels of existence, including the *Asuras*, the great mental beings who are a challenge to any godlike powers, the *rakshasas*, who are comparable to the titans in Greek mythology, and the *pishachas*, the small beings on the lowest vital levels who have pleasure in making the lives of the humans and of each other as chaotic as possible.

"Imagine not the way is easy", wrote Sri Aurobindo from experience, "the way is long, arduous, dangerous, difficult. At every step is an ambush, at every turn a pitfall. A thousand seen or unseen enemies will start up against thee, terrible in subtlety against thy ignorance, formidable in power against thy weakness. And when with pain thou hast destroyed them, other thousands will surge up to take their place. Hell will vomit its hordes to oppose thee with its pitiless tests and its cold luminous denials. Thou shalt find thyself alone in thy anguish, the demons furious in thy path, the Gods unwilling above thee. Ancient and powerful, cruel, unvanquished and close and innumerable are the dark and dreadful Powers that profit by the reign of Night and Ignorance and would have no change and are hostile. Aloof, slow to arrive, far-off and few and brief in visits are the Bright Ones who are willing or permitted to succour.

## 6. The Supramental "Catastrophe"

Each step forward is a battle."[44] "None can reach heaven who has not passed through hell,"[45] he wrote in *Savitri*.

> There is no visible foe, but the unseen
> Is round us, forces intangible besiege,
> Touches from alien realms, thoughts not our own
> Overtake us and compel the erring heart;
> Our lives are caught in an ambiguous net.
> An adversary Force was born of old:
> Invader of the life of mortal man,
> It hides from him the straight immortal path.[46]

Our second marginal note is about the children. From 1967 onwards the Mother said that many of the newborn children were special, particularly the children of parents in some way or other related to the ongoing evolutionary transformation. "Since a few months the children born, amongst our people mainly, are of a very special kind."[47] And four years later she said: "I really think that it is among the children that there are those able to begin the new race."[48] It is now often observed that the new generation of children is amazingly intelligent,[49] that they seem to be fully aware of themselves and have the gift of looking straight through you. It is for this sort of children that the Mother founded her school with its integral education, based on the theory and practice of the Integral Yoga. She warned that children born with a special mission, mature souls all of them, might be difficult to understand and educate, and that much patience was needed to accompany them during the first years of their life. Generally unrecognised, they are

---

44. Sri Aurobindo: *Essays Divine and Human*, pp. 155-56.
45. Sri Aurobindo: *Savitri*, p.227.
46. Id., p. 447.
47. *Words of the Mother*, CWM 15, p. 113.
48. The Mother: *Notes on the Way*, p. 252.
49. A six year old boy, while being bathed by his mother: "Mammy, there are people who think that God is a 'he', but they know nothing about it. And there are others who think that God is a 'she', but they know nothing either." (Joanne Klink: *Vroeger, toen ik groot was* – In bygone years, when I was big – p. 128).

155

among the overmen and overwomen of the present. They are the hope of the future, not vaguely or sentimentally as is so often expressed in solemn speeches on ceremonious occasions, but concretely, effectively.

> I saw the Omnipotent's flaming pioneers
> Over the heavenly verge which turns towards life
> Come crowding down the amber stairs of birth;
> Forerunners of a divine multitude,
> Out of the paths of the morning star they came
> Into the little room of mortal life.
> I saw them cross the twilight of an age,
> The sun-eyed children of a marvellous dawn,
> The great creators with wide brows of calm,
> The massive barrier-breakers of the world
> And wrestlers with destiny in her lists of will,
> The labourers in the quarries of the gods,
> The messengers of the Incommunicable,
> The architects of immortality.[50]

## *The Four Aids of the Overman*

"Imagine not the way is easy ..." The reader may remember Sri Aurobindo's poem *A God's Labour*, in which he writes about his avataric ordeals; a testimony of what the Mother went through can be found in some of her conversations in *Mother's Agenda*. The world does not yet realise the scope and the difficulty of their avataric *sadhana*, nor scarcely do their followers. They repeatedly said that their labour would make the path easier or possible for those following them, but "easier" does not mean "easy".

The difficulty of the path makes us understand why those who want to follow it have to be called to it. It is not an aim one can set oneself by a simple mental decision; the dedication to such

---

50. Sri Aurobindo: *Savitri*, pp. 343-44.

## 6. The Supramental "Catastrophe"

an aim can only be the consequence of an increasing aspiration throughout many lives, a selfless dedication to share the divine Work in the manifestation. This also explains why "surrender" is "the Alpha and the Omega" of the Integral Yoga: the souls who have given themselves to it cannot expect the realisation of the goal in this lifetime, because the goal of the Integral Yoga is the supramental transformation, which can only be reached after centuries. The second reason is that nobody can practice the Integral Yoga for selfish aims. A necessary condition of the supramental transformation is the acquisition of the cosmic consciousness, something that is impossible in the ego-state. Besides, the acquisition of the supramental consciousness, even in a single cell of a human body, is a cosmic event with repercussions throughout the cosmos. "We want a race without ego ..."

All this would be unattainable without the four supramental aids, totally new in the history of spirituality.

1. *The presence of the Supermind.* Thanks to the avataric *sadhana* of Sri Aurobindo and the Mother the supramental Consciousness was established in the earth-atmosphere on 29 February 1956. This date marks the exact end of the old world order and the beginning of the new. "This is becoming more and more true from day to day, from hour to hour: the feeling that this [supramental] Force, when it is directed by what we call 'the Divine', that it *can*, it truly *can* – you understand? It has the power to make Matter move. It can produce a *material* event, and it can efface the consequences of an absolutely material event: it is stronger than Matter. This is what is altogether new and incomprehensible, and therefore it produces a kind of bewilderment in the ordinary consciousness of people ... *It is no longer as it was.* Truly, there is something new: *it is no longer as it was*. All our common sense, all our logic, all our practical sense is dashed to the ground – useless! It has no force any more, no reality. It no longer corresponds to what is. This truly is a new world ...

"But there is one essential condition: the reign of the ego must have come to an end. The ego is now the obstacle. The ego must be replaced by the divine Consciousness. Sri Aurobindo called it 'Supermind'. We too can call it 'Supermind' so that there is no misunderstanding. Because when one speaks of 'the Divine', people immediately think of a 'God', and that spoils everything. It is not that. No, it is not that: it is the descent of the supramental world, which is not merely something of the imagination. It is an *absolutely material* Power, but it has no need of material things. A world that wants to incarnate within the world."[51]

In 1954 the Mother had already mentioned a change in the composition of gross Matter, perceptible in the presence of particles which had all the colours of the rainbow. In the course of the transformation of her body she will mention this changed Matter more and more often. The body of the supramental being cannot consist of the same substance as ours. Gross Matter is the direct outcome of the Inconscient; therefore a supramentally conscious body can only incarnate in a transformed, supramentalised substance. It was this supramentalisation of Matter that she perceived.

"This manner of being is still very undefinable. In this research, though, there is a constant perception, translated by a vision, of a multicoloured light comprising all the colours – all the colours not in layers but as though *(gesture of dotting)* as if connected by dots of every colour. It is now two years – perhaps a little more, I don't remember any more – since I met the Tantrics. I was in relation with them and I started seeing this light, and I thought that it was the 'tantric light', the tantric way of seeing the material world. But now I see it constantly, in relation with everything, and it seems to be what one might call a perception of 'true Matter'. All possible colours are connected without being intermingled *(same gesture of dotting)*, and connected by luminous dots. Everything is made of that, as it were. And this seems to be the true manner of being. I am not yet sure, but in any case it is a much more conscious manner of being."

And the Mother painstakingly tried to describe her perception

---

51. The Mother: *Notes on the Way*, pp. 315 ff. (emphasis in the text).

## 6. The Supramental "Catastrophe"

of this new substance: "And I see it all the time: with eyes open, with eyes closed – all the time. And one has a strange – for the body, that is – a strange perception at once of subtleness, of penetrability if one may say so, of suppleness of the form and positively not of an eradication but a considerable diminution in the rigidity of the forms. Eradication of rigidity, not eradication of the forms: a suppleness in the forms. And when the body for the first time felt this in one part or another, it had the impression – it felt somewhat confused – the impression that something was escaping [from its control]. But if one keeps very quiet and waits quietly, that is simply replaced by a sort of plasticity, of fluidity, which for the cells seems a new way of being."[52]

2. *The presence of the Consciousness of the Overman.* The manifestation and the first workings of the Consciousness of the Overman have been extensively described elsewhere.[53] Let us recall that it is a special formation of the supramental Consciousness intended to bring about the appearance of the transitional species or various kinds of transitional beings between man and superman. It continued being active after January 1969: the Mother mentioned it throughout the remaining years of her life, and she was always grateful for its presence and guidance.

"My impression was that of an immense personality – immense!" the Mother said when trying to describe this consciousness for the first time. "By this I mean that the earth was small for it, small like this *(gesture as if holding a little ball in the palm of her hand)*, like a ball. An immense personality, very, very benevolent, that came for *(the Mother seems to lift the little ball gently from the palm of her hand)*. It gave the impression of a personal divinity who comes to help. And so strong, so strong! and at the same time so gentle, so all-embracing."[54]

"It is a guide. It is a consciousness, after all ... Strange, it is as if I were given the task of putting it into contact with all

---

52. Id., pp. 57-58.
53. See Georges Van Vrekhem: *Overman: The Intermediary between the Human and the Supramental Being* (Rupa & Co).
54. Id., pp. 149-50.

those who come near me,"[55] the Mother said. Afterwards she often mentioned the practical guidance of this Overman Consciousness, glad that she had found some concrete assistance on her perilous adventure in "the virgin forest", where as yet there was no beaten path. "Many of the activities [of her avataric yoga] I have left to this Consciousness", she said in 1970. "I let this Consciousness work actively because I found that it really knows."[56]

It is this Consciousness of the Overman, an activated aspect of the Supramental Consciousness adapted to the present circumstances, which is at work now. It is changing the world through its formation and guidance of beings who are open to it, the overmen and overwomen. The turmoil of the present world in which we live is caused by this Consciousness – to which the ongoing change is not an unpredictable vortex, but a process guided in the smallest details. Before the descent of the Supermind the transformation of the lower into the higher hemisphere was a certainty, for the Avatar never comes without accomplishing his mission, but the way in which it would come about could not be foreseen, as Sri Aurobindo said so often. At the very moment of the manifestation of the Supermind the process of the supramental transformation of our world was initiated, but it could still take "thousands of years". The *sadhana* of the Mother induced the Consciousness of the Overman, which manifested on 1 January 1969 and effected the unseen presence among humanity of the first overmen and overwomen. Through them is worked out the guidance of the Overman Consciousness, which is sometimes detectable in the world events.

3. *The presence of Sri Aurobindo.* Death is a laying down of the physical body by the soul. The soul remains "sheathed" in its vital and mental bodies to the extent that these have been developed. But what happens if the vital and mental sheaths are supramentalised? Supramentalisation means divinisation

---

55. Every being is a consciousness, every consciousness is a being.
56. The Mother: *Notes on the Way*, p. 241.

## 6. The Supramental "Catastrophe"

which means immortality. Sri Aurobindo's vital and mental sheaths had been supramentalised for many years when he entered voluntarily into death with all his conscious powers. This means that he exists in a supramentalised vital and mental body somewhere in a corresponding supramental world. The Mother often referred to "Sri Aurobindo's abode" in "the subtle physical", i.e. in a supramental world[57] where she and many of the followers still among the living went to visit him, and where some of the disciples who had left their body stayed with him, in his company.

In 1953 the Mother wrote in a letter: "[Sri Aurobindo] has not left me, not for a moment – for He is still with me, day and night, thinking through my brain, writing through my pen, speaking through my mouth and acting through my organising power."[58] She would often report his presence with her – "he is here all the time" – or in the Ashram (especially on *darshan* days), and his advice or decisions, his interventions in world situations. "I see now", she said in 1970, "I see how his departure and his work so vast, yes, and so constant in the subtle physical, how much, how much it has helped! How much it has helped to prepare things, to change the physical structure."[59] And two years later: "He himself has more action, more power for action, now than when he was in his body. Besides, it is for this reason that he left, because it was necessary to do so. It is very concrete, you see, his action has become very concrete. Evidently it is something that is not mental at all, it is from another region. But it is not ethereal nor ... It is concrete. One could almost say that it is material."[60]

One of the many statements and messages the Mother gave after Sri Aurobindo's passing was the following: "In the eternity of becoming, each Avatar is only the announcer, the forerunner

---

57. See for example *Mother's Agenda*, 6 October 1959. The "subtle physical" is in fact an occult gradation of the physical or material, but in the years after her withdrawal the Mother used this term more and more for the supramental, especially when concretely perceived.
58. *Champaklal Speaks*, 251.
59. The Mother: *Notes on the Way*, p. 229.
60. Id., p. 329.

of a more perfect realisation. And yet men have always the tendency to deify the Avatar of the past in opposition to the Avatar of the future. Now again Sri Aurobindo has come announcing to the world the realisation of tomorrow; and again his message meets with the same opposition as of all those who preceded him. But tomorrow will prove the truth of what he revealed and his work will be done."

4. *The presence of the Mother.* From 1950 till 1958 the Mother worked at realising the *surhomme*: overman. Let us recall what she said close to the achievement of this realisation: "It is quite obvious that intermediary beings are necessary, and that it is these intermediary beings who must find the means to create beings of the Supermind. And there is no doubt that, when Sri Aurobindo wrote this, he was convinced that this is what we have to do. I think – I know – that it is now certain that we shall realise what he expects of us. It is no longer a hope, it is a certainty." Towards the end of 1958 she withdrew to the second floor of the central Ashram building in Rue de la Marine in order to take up the following phase of her sadhana: the transformation of her human body into a supramental body. What this attempt meant, we have a glimpse of in the volumes of *Mother's Agenda,* her conversations with a French disciple, and in *Notes on the Way,* extracts from these conversations published in the Ashram's *Bulletin of Physical Education* from 1965 onwards.

On 24 March 1972, the Mother reported: "For the first time, early in the morning, I saw myself, my body. I do not know whether it is the supramental body or – how to say it? – a transitional body. But I had a body completely new in the sense that it was sexless: it was neither a woman nor was it a man. It was very white, but this is because my skin is white, I think, I don't know. It was very slim. It was beautiful, really a harmonious form. So, this was the first time. I did not know at all. I had no idea how it would be like or whatever, and I saw: I was like that, I had become like that."

The next day she returned to the subject: "I was like that. It was myself. I did not see myself in a mirror: I saw myself like the *(Mother bends her head down)* ... I did not look to see how it was

## 6. The Supramental "Catastrophe"

because everything happened quite naturally, so I cannot give a detailed description. Simply, it was neither the body of a woman nor the body of a man, that much is clear. And *the outline* [in English in the text], the silhouette, was almost the same, as of a very, very young person. There was as it were the remembrance of the human forms: there was a shoulder and a waist. The remembrance of a form, as it were ... I saw it in the way one sees oneself. And there was a kind of veil that I had put on, like this, to cover myself. It was not surprising to me: it was a natural way of being. It must be like that in the subtle physical."[61]

Without going into details, let us consider the following. A transitional body, generated as all bodies are now, is not sexless. As the body the Mother saw was sexless, it must have been a supramental body, for this is how she said the supramental body would be. At the time she saw her new body, "as of a very, very young person", she was ninety-four. What she called "the subtle physical" in her conversations, she sometimes also called "the true physical" and used this term to locate "Sri Aurobindo's abode" in the supramental. Putting these elements together – and there are more – there is little doubt that the Mother had built a supramental body that would be the prototype or archetype of the supramental bodies to come. With the descent of the Supermind, the establishment of the Overman Consciousness and the realisation of the prototype of the supramental body all the foundations were laid for the development of the New World.

This also means that, like Sri Aurobindo, the Mother lives in an immortal body. Hers is even more fully supramental than Sri Aurobindo's because not only the mental and vital sheaths of her *adhara* were supramentalised, but also part of the material sheath. (This is what most of her conversations from 1958 till 1973, recorded in the *Agenda,* were about.) Consequently she, like him, is omnipresent in a supramental form, doubtlessly always there to ensure the progress of the Work and help the souls who are dedicating their present incarnation to it.

---

61. The Mother: *Notes on the Way,* pp. 302 ff. (emphasis in the text).

## The Avataric Interaction with History

> There already have been for many years extraordinary, fantastic consequences [of the avataric Yoga] in the world. An action in the world? It is constant. But to see it, one must have some knowledge. Otherwise one believes them to be quite normal and ordinary events, because one doesn't even know how they happen.[62]
>
> – THE MOTHER

> We are living in a new world, a world that does not know how to define itself by what it is, but only by what it has just-now ceased to be.[63]
>
> – WALTER TRUETT ANDERSON

The exceptional individual that is the Vibhuti comes to accomplish a specific action in the evolution of mankind; the divine individual that is the Avatar comes to accomplish something essential for the evolution of mankind. Parasurama stood at the origin of *homo habilis* or represents him symbolically; Rama incarnated the rational mind and thus generated the possibility of *homo sapiens*. The influence of the mission of Krishna and the Buddha remained limited to Asia for centuries, till it eventually spread over the whole globe. The avataric, Integral Yoga of Sri Aurobindo and the Mother was in principle intended for the transformation of humanity, and must therefore have had global consequences in their lifetime and afterwards.

India has become free; Asia has woken up; in Europe the European Union has been founded; the world is becoming one; Indian spirituality is penetrating the West; the supramental transformation of the world is under way. Each of these momentous changes in history was predicted by Sri Aurobindo between 1914 and 1921, at a moment in history when they not only seemed implausible but outright impossible. And Sri Aurobindo

---

62. The Mother: *Questions and Answers 1956*, pp. 10-11.
63. In *The Fontana Postmodernism Reader*, p. 6.

## 6. The Supramental "Catastrophe"

did not "predict" or "foresee" these historical milestones in the way seers or clairvoyants do: he formulated their rationale and described their probable way of coming about in great detail. His two books dealing with these topics are *The Human Cycle* and *The Ideal of Human Unity*, but his concern with them is present everywhere in his writings, for the fulfilment of these historic evolutions was (and is) required for the accomplishment of the supramental transformation.[64]

We need not go further into the subject of INDIA'S FREEDOM here. Sri Aurobindo was the first to formulate the need of India's unconditional freedom. His concern with his motherland and its culture is evident throughout his work, specifically in writings like The Renaissance *of India, The Secret of the Veda, Essays on the Gita, Writings in Bengali,* articles from *Bande Mataram* and the *Karmayogin*, etc. The Mother said that India was "the country of her soul".

About ASIA, Sri Aurobindo wrote: "We have then to return to the pursuit of the ancient secret which man, as a race, has seen only obscurely and followed after lamely, has indeed understood only with his surface mind and not in its heart of meaning, – and yet in following it lies his social no less than his individual salvation, – the ideal of the Kingdom of God, the secret of the reign of the Spirit over mind and life and body. It is because they have never quite lost hold of this secret, never disowned it in impatience for a lesser victory, that the older Asiatic nations have survived so persistently and can now, as if immortal, raise their faces towards a new dawn; for they have fallen asleep, but they have not perished."[65] This was written in 1915. It may be

---

64. Ken Wilber is one of the most interesting synthetic thinkers of the present moment. In his *Integral Psychology* (1999) he writes, however: "Although [Sri Aurobindo] had many important insights on the social and political system, he did not seem to grasp the actual interrelations of [the] cultural, social, intentional, and behavioural, nor did his analysis at any point proceed on the level of intersubjectivity ... and interobjectivity ..." This raises the question of what Wilber has actually read of Sri Aurobindo besides *The Life Divine*.
65. Sri Aurobindo: *The Human Cycle*, p. 239.

considered a fact that Asia, whatever its problems, has woken up since then.

Sri Aurobindo deemed it imperative that in the future global development groups of countries, bound by historical and cultural interests or relations, would unite in supranational structures. That this was prescient is proven by the South-Asian SAARC and ASEAN, the American OAS, the African OAU, the ever closer ties between the countries on the Pacific Rim – and of course especially by the still expanding EUROPEAN UNION. "Some form of European federation, however loose, is therefore essential if the idea behind these suggestions of a new order is to be made practically effective, and once commenced, such a federation must necessarily be tightened and draw more and more towards the form of a United States of Europe."[66]

In a "Postscript Chapter" to his *Ideal of Human Unity,* Sri Aurobindo wrote in April 1950: "One of the possibilities suggested at the time [of writing *The Ideal of Human Unity*] was the growth of continental agglomerates, a united Europe, some kind of a combine of the peoples of the American continent under the leadership of the United States, even possibly the resurgence of Asia and its drive towards independence from the dominance of the European peoples, a drawing together for a self-defensive combination of the nations of this continent; such an eventuality of large continental combinations might even be a stage in the final formation of a world-union. This possibility has tended to take shape to a certain extent with a celerity that could not then be anticipated. In the two American continents it has actually assumed a predominating and practical form, though not in the totality. The idea of a United States of Europe has also actually taken shape and is assuming a formal existence, but is not yet able to develop into a completed and fully realised possibility because of the antagonism based on conflicting ideologies which cuts off from each other Russia and her satellites behind their iron curtain and Western Europe. This separation has gone so far that it is difficult to envisage its

---

66. Sri Aurobindo: *The Human Cycle,* p. 351.

## 6. The Supramental "Catastrophe"

cessation at any foreseeable time in a predictable future."⁶⁷ At present three of Russia's former satellites are member states of the European Union ...

An important aspect of Sri Aurobindo and the Mother's Work was the building up of a global unity, a WORLD-UNION. According to them, the unification (in diversity) of humanity was an essential requisite for the supramental realisation. The following quotations will speak more eloquently than any comment can do.

- "Mankind upon earth is one foremost self-expression of the universal Being in His cosmic self-unfolding; he expresses, under the conditions of the terrestrial world he inhabits, the mental power of the universal existence. All mankind is one in its nature, physical, vital, emotional, mental and ever has been in spite of all differences of intellectual development ranging from the poverty of the bushman and Negroid to the rich cultures of Asia and Europe, and the whole race has, as the human totality, one destiny which it seeks and increasingly approaches in the cycles of progression and retrogression it describes through the countless millenniums of its history. Nothing which any individual race or nation can triumphantly realise, no victory of their self-aggrandisement, illumination, intellectual achievement or mastery over the environment has any permanent meaning or value except in so far as it adds something or recovers something or preserves something for this human march."⁶⁸

- "The collective being is a fact; all mankind may be regarded as a collective being: but this being is a soul and life, not merely a mind and a body."⁶⁹

- "[Individual man] is not merely the noble, merchant, warrior, priest, scholar, artist, cultivator or artisan, not merely the religionist or the worldling or the politician. Nor can

---
67. Id., p. 590.
68. Id., p. 67.
69. Id., p. 210.

he be limited by his nationality; he is not merely the Englishman or the Frenchman, the Japanese or the Indian; if by a part of himself he belongs to the nation, by another he exceeds it and belongs to humanity. And even there is a part in him the greatest, which is not limited by humanity; he belongs by it to God and to the world of all beings and to the godheads of the future."[70]

- "The perfect society will be that which most entirely favours the perfection of the individual; the perfection of the individual will be incomplete if it does not help towards the perfect state of the social aggregate to which he belongs and eventually to that of the largest possible human aggregate, the whole of a united humanity."[71]

- "Today the ideal of human unity is more or less vaguely making its way to the front of our consciousness ... The ideal, having once made its way to the front of thought, must certainly be attempted, and this ideal of human unity is likely to figure largely among the determining forces of the future; for the intellectual and material circumstances of the age have prepared and almost impose it, especially the scientific discoveries which have made our earth so small that its vastest kingdoms seem now no more than the provinces of a single country."[72]

- "The earth is in travail now of one common, large and flexible civilisation for the whole human race into which each modern and ancient culture shall bring its contribution and each clearly defined human aggregate shall introduce its necessary element of variation."[73]

- "Perhaps liberty and equality, liberty and authority, liberty and organised efficiency can never be quite satisfactorily reconciled as long as man individual and aggregate lives

---
70. Id., p. 69.
71. Id., p. 285.
72. Id., p. 285.
73. Id., p. 319.

## 6. The Supramental "Catastrophe"

by egoism, so long as he cannot undergo a great spiritual and psychological change and rise beyond mere communal association to that third ideal which some vague inner sense made the revolutionary thinkers of France add to their watchwords of liberty and equality, – the greatest of all the three, though till now only an empty word on man's lips, the ideal of fraternity or, less sentimentally and more truly expressed, an inner oneness. That no mechanism social, political, religious has ever created or can create; it must take birth in the soul and rise from hidden and divine depths within."[74]

- "Continent has no longer a separate life from continent; no nation can any longer isolate itself at will and live a separate existence. Science, commerce and rapid communications have produced a state of things in which the disparate masses of humanity, once living to themselves, have been drawn together by a process of subtle unification into a single mass which has already a common vital and is rapidly forming a common mental existence. A great precipitating and transforming shock was needed which should make this subtle organic unity manifest and reveal the necessity and create the will for a closer and organised union and this shock came with the Great War [i.e. the First World War]. The idea of a World-State or world-union has been born not only in the speculating forecasting mind of the thinker but in the consciousness of humanity out of the very necessity of this new common existence. The World-State must now either be brought about by a mutual understanding or by the force of circumstances and a series of new and disastrous shocks."[75]

- "Mankind has a habit of surviving the worst catastrophes created by its own errors or by the violent turns of Nature and it must be so if there is any meaning in its existence, if

---
74. Id., p. 383.
75. Id., p. 463.

its long history and continuous survival is not the accident of a fortuitously self-organising Chance, which it must be in a purely materialistic view of the nature of the world. If man is intended to survive and carry forward the evolution of which he is at present the head and, to some extent, a half-conscious leader of its march, he must come out of his present chaotic international life and arrive at a beginning of organised united action; some kind of World-State, unitary or federal, or a confederacy or a coalition he must arrive at in the end; no smaller or looser expedient would adequately serve the purpose."[76]

- "An authority of this nature [then the League of Nations, now the United Nations] would have to command the psychological assent of mankind, exercise a moral force upon the nations greater than that of their own national authority and compel more readily their obedience under all normal circumstances. It would have not only to be a symbol and a centre of the unity of the race but make itself constantly serviceable to the world by assuring the effective maintenance and development of large common interests and benefits which would outweigh all separate national interests and satisfy entirely the sense of need that had brought it into existence. It must help more and more to fix the growing sense of a common humanity and a common life in which the sharp divisions which separate country from country, race from race, colour from colour, continent from continent would gradually lose their force and undergo a progressive effacement. Given these conditions, it would develop a moral authority which would enable it to pursue with less and less opposition and friction the unification of mankind."[77]

Sri Aurobindo's next prediction was about INDIAN SPIRITUALITY spreading to the West and the other parts of the globe. That

---
76. Id., p. 585.
77. Id., p. 482.

## 6. The Supramental "Catastrophe"

this has become a fact, and is ever-increasing, is so obvious that it does not need documentary support. The start of this contact – the fourth enrichment of the West by the Eastern spirit according to Sri Aurobindo – may be taken to be 1893, the year Vivekananda was sent to the USA by Ramakrishna Paramhansa in order to participate in the Congress of World Religions at Chicago. "No one could have imagined then that a Hindu monk would make converts in London and Chicago or that a Vedantic temple would be built in San Francisco and Anglo-Saxon Islamites erect a Musulman mosque in Liverpool", noted Sri Aurobindo in 1912.[78] Nor could anyone have imagined then that by the end of the 20th century about 300,000 French and 250,000 Dutch would be practising Buddhists. "That which is permanent in the Hindu religion, must form the basis on which the world will increasingly take its stand in dealing with spiritual experience and religious truth,"[79] wrote Sri Aurobindo. And "that which is permanent in the Hindu religion" may well prove to be the synthesis he and the Mother first realised and then formulated.

It has already been stated in one of the previous chapters that there is a fundamental flaw at the basis of the whole body of modern Western thought: the distorted picture of the human being constructed by modern Western philosophy and psychology as a consequence of and a reaction against the Christian Middle Ages. If the Chain of Being – the universal hierarchy or gradations of being – was recognised at all, it was only felt as theoretical, never as real. The West took an instrument of consciousness, rational mind or Reason, as the *nec plus ultra;* it based itself on the immediate given, Matter, and never investigated life and the supra-rational levels and worlds from which, after all, its seminal inspirations came. The idea of the soul, which generally had remained very misty, was discarded by science, as were all matters occult and religious – but only up to a certain point. For it is touching when studying the history of Marxism,

---
78. Sri Aurobindo: *Essays Divine and Human, p. 192.*
79. Id., p. 59.

Fascism, Nazism, Russian communism and Maoism, among other national or worldwide movements, to see how desperately millions of people have been surrendering themselves to these pseudo-religions. Now, even the blessings of consumerism cannot fill up "the hole within".

The fifth prediction and practical endeavour of Sri Aurobindo and the Mother was the SUPRAMENTAL TRANSFORMATION of matter and of humanity. For this the reader may refer to my aforementioned books.

> As yet thought only some high spirit's dream
> Or a vexed illusion in man's toiling mind,
> A new creation from the old shall rise,
> A knowledge inarticulate find speech,
> Beauty suppressed burst into paradise bloom,
> Pleasure and pain dive into absolute bliss.
> A tongueless oracle shall speak at last,
> The Superconscient conscious grow on earth,
> The Eternal's wonder join the dance of Time.[80]

## Impact upon History

In March 1958 the Mother said: "One thing seems obvious: humanity has reached such a state of general tension – tension in its endeavour, tension in its action, tension even in its daily life – with such an excessive hyperactivity, such a widespread trepidation, that the species as a whole seems to have come to a point where it must either break through the resistance and emerge into a new consciousness or else fall back into an abyss of obscurity and inertia.

"This tension is so total and has become so generalised that obviously something has to break. It cannot go on in this way. We may take it as a sure sign of the infusion into matter of a new principle of force, of consciousness, of power, that by its

---

80. Sri Aurobindo: *Savitri*, p. 330.

## 6. The Supramental "Catastrophe"

very pressure produces this acute state. Outwardly we would expect the old methods used by Nature when she wants to bring about a violent change. There is however a new characteristic, of course only visible in an élite, but even this élite is sufficiently widespread. It is not localised at one point, at one place in the world; one finds clues of it in all countries, on the whole earth: the will to find a new, progressive, higher solution, an effort to rise towards a larger, more comprehensive perfection.

"Certain ideas of a more general nature, of a wider, one could say more 'collective' kind, are being worked out and acting in the world. And both things go together: a possibility of a greater and more total destruction, a recklessness which increases the possibility of catastrophe beyond all limits, a catastrophe which would be far greater than ever before; and at the same time the birth or rather the manifestation of much higher and more comprehensive ideas and acts of the will which, when they are listened to, will bring a larger, more comprehensive, more complete, more perfect solution than before.

"This struggle, this conflict between the constructive forces of the ascending evolution, of a more and more perfect and divine realisation, and the ever more destructive – wildly destructive, forces of a madness beyond all control – is more and more evident, noticeable, visible, and it is a kind of race or of a struggle as to which [of the two sides] will reach its goal first. It would seem that all the adverse, antidivine forces, the forces of the vital world, have descended upon the earth, that they are using it as their fields of action,[81] and that at the same time a new, higher, more powerful spiritual force has also descended on earth to bring it a new life. This renders the struggle more acute, more violent, more visible, but also, it seems, more definitive, and that is why we can hope to reach an early solution.

"There was a time, not so long ago, when the spiritual

---

81. Sri Aurobindo and the Mother often said that the lower, dark vital forces had made a massive inrush upon the Earth during the First World War. "The First World War was the result of tremendous descent of the vital forces – the hostile forces of the vital world – into the material world." (The Mother: *Questions and Answers 1953*, p. 184).

aspiration of man was turned towards a silent, inactive peace, detached from all worldly things, a flight from life, precisely in order to avoid battle, to rise above all struggle, to escape from all effort ... In fact, no matter what one wants to realise, one must begin by establishing this perfect and immutable peace. It is the basis from which one must work. But unless one dreams of an exclusive, personal and egoistic liberation, one cannot stop there. There is another aspect of the divine Grace, the aspect of a progress that will be victorious of all obstacles, the aspect that will propel humanity towards a new realisation, that will open the doors of a new world, that will make it possible that not only a chosen few will benefit from the divine realisation, but that their influence, their example, their power will bring new and better conditions to the rest of mankind. This opens up roads of realisation into the future, possibilities which are already foreseen, when an entire part of humanity, the whole part that has opened itself consciously or unconsciously to the new forces, is lifted up, as it were, into a higher, more harmonious, more perfect life."[82]

The impact of the lives of the Avatar of the Supermind, or rather the interaction between his/her avataric *sadhana* and history is a subject still to be examined in detail. A few facts are nevertheless very telling, while others are rather suggestive in this direction. That the First World War began at the moment the *Arya* was published and the Second World Way at the time of the publication of *The Life Divine*, however significant, may be taken as a coincidence – though according to Sri Aurobindo and the Mother coincidences do not exist: everything hangs together in the manifestation of the All.

The impact of the avataric *sadhana* upon history becomes unmistakable in the 1930s, when the rise of Nazism paralleled the curve of Sri Aurobindo's effort to bring down the Supermind. The whole process can be followed almost step by step in Nirodbaran's *Correspondence with Sri Aurobindo*. Hidden behind Nazism and causing its success was the action of the Asura of

---

82. The Mother: *Questions and Answers 1957-58,* pp. 296 ff.

## 6. The Supramental "Catastrophe"

Falsehood who calls himself "the Lord of the Nations"[83]. In 1938, when the descent of the Supermind seemed imminent, Sri Aurobindo was directly attacked and broke his thigh. That the Second World War was intended to countermand the mission of the Avatar has been stated explicitly by Sri Aurobindo as well as by the Mother.

"I affirm again to you most strongly that this is the Mother's war", wrote Sri Aurobindo to an Indian disciple when circumstances were critical. "You should not think of it as a fight for certain nations against others or even for India; it is a struggle for an ideal that has to establish itself on earth in the life of humanity, for a Truth that has yet to realise itself fully and against a darkness and falsehood that are trying to overwhelm the earth and mankind in the immediate future. It is the forces behind the battle that have to be seen and not this or that superficial circumstance ... It is a struggle for the liberty of mankind to develop, for conditions in which men have freedom and room to think and act according to the light in them and grow in the Truth, grow in the Spirit ..."[84]

"The victory of one side (the Allies) would keep the path open for the evolutionary forces: the victory of the other side would drag back humanity, degrade it horribly and might lead even, at the worst, to its eventual failure as a race, as others in the past evolution failed and perished. That is the whole question and all other considerations are either irrelevant or of a minor importance. The Allies at least have stood for human values, though they may often act against their own best ideals (human beings always do that); Hitler stands for diabolical values or for human values exaggerated in the wrong way until they become diabolical ..."[85]

The struggle for the liberty of mankind was fought and won, but the end of the world war did not mean the end of the activities of the Lord of Falsehood. In June 1950, a few months before his departure, Sri Aurobindo wrote in a note to K.D.

---

83. See the relevant chapters in *Beyond Man* and *Mother*.
84. Sri Aurobindo: *On Himself*, p. 394.
85. Id., p. 396.

*Patterns of the Present*

Sethna on the Korean War: "The whole affair is as plain as a pike-staff. It is the move in the Communist plan of campaign to dominate and take possession first of these northern parts [including Korea] and then of South East Asia as a preliminary to their manoeuvres with regard to the rest of the continent – in passing, Tibet as a gate opening to India. If they succeed, there is no reason why domination of the whole world should not follow by steps until they are ready to deal with America ... If America gives up now her defence of Korea, she may be driven to yield position after position until it is too late: at one point or another she will have to stand and face the necessity of drastic action even if it leads to war ... For the moment the situation is as grave as it can be."[86]

1955 was a peak year in the Cold War, as it was also the year of the Bandung Conference where recently decolonialised powers of the "Third World" stood up together against the Capitalist and Communist Blocs. About 1955 the Mother said: "It is the last hope of the adverse forces to triumph against the present Realisation. If we [i.e. the people who practise the Integral Yoga] can stand firm during these months, they won't be able to do much afterwards, their resistance will crumble. This is what it is about: it is the essential conflict of the adverse forces, of the antidivine forces, who are trying to push back the divine Realisation as much as possible – thousands of years, they hope. And it is this conflict that has reached its paroxysm. It is their last chance. And as the beings that are behind their exterior action are totally conscious, they are fully aware that it is their last chance, and they will do everything they can. And what they can is quite a lot."[87] The Mother had earlier reminded her audience what a tremendous catastrophe and evolutionary setback is the wiping out of a civilisation. In 1955, and of course in the following decades, the superpowers had the capacity to erase the present civilisations and even the whole of humanity from the globe. That this did not happen, taking into account "what

---

86. Id., p. 417.
87. The Mother: *Questions and Answers 1954*, p. 523.

## 6. The Supramental "Catastrophe"

human beings always do", is one of the mysteries of history that may only be explainable from the Aurobindonian angle. Then, in 1956, the Supermind descended into the earth-atmosphere. Its descent meant the certitude of the coming of the supramental species. A new world was born.

The Mother often mentioned the action of the new supramental Force in the world. This action became quite obvious in the 1960s, the decade of which the importance has been continually growing in the historians' estimation, so much so that according to some of them history has become an interpreter's problem from that time onwards.

A new spirit was spreading over the Earth calling the whole Western paradigm into question. The most colourful exponents of this new spirit were America's "flower children", soon imitated by "hippies" everywhere. Whatever the confusion, inevitable on the fault-line between two worlds, the sincerity of their inspiration and of their peaceful protest against values gone stale is undeniable. They represented, according to Luc Ferry, "a vision of the world characterised by a claim to 'authenticity' and demanding, in the name of the respect of the individual, the eradication of all dogmatisms whether of moral or religious origin."[88]

In their search for authenticity, the flower children spontaneously focused on forms of thought and spiritual practice in relation to the big gap in Western philosophy, psychology and religion: the spiritual life, the soul. For this they turned towards the East, and firstly, towards India. "According to what I am being told", said the Mother in 1964, "I mean by people who listen to the radio and read the newspapers – things that I do not do – the whole world seems to be undergoing an action which for the moment is upsetting. It seems that the number of those who are apparently mad increases considerably. In America, for example, the entire youth seems to be in the grip of a kind of curious vertigo which may be disquieting to reasonable people, but which is certainly an indication that an unusual force is at

---

88. Luc Ferry: *L'Homme-Dieu*, p. 84.

work. It means the breaking of all the habits and all the rules. It is good. For the moment it is rather strange, but it is necessary."[89]

Then came "May '68", the culmination of that bizarre decade – just after the founding of Auroville by the Mother. May '68 started in Paris, but it spread like wildfire among the young people of the whole world, and it is certainly legitimate to count the "Prague Spring", the revolt in Czechoslovakia against the Russian form of communism, as an aspect of that movement. "A radical irruption of the new", "a new period in universal history", "a revolt of the individuals against the norms, in the sense of the affirmation of the individuality against the pretension of the norms to be universal", write the commentators.[90] "The principal representatives of the thought of '68 have made history without knowing what history they were making." "The actors of May were actually the inconscient agents of a process by which they were encompassed and surpassed."

From the Aurobindonian standpoint there is little doubt that the spirit which took possession of the youth in 1968 and animated them with a quest for authenticity, was the direct outflow of the new Force present in the world, and very probably a consequence of the special Force the Mother had applied for the foundation of Auroville, the utopian "City of Dawn", founded by her to be a field of experimentation for the creation of the new being. The charter of Auroville, formulated by the Mother, and the slogans of May'68 in Paris are worth a comparative study. The whole "elan" of May '68 tells of a thirst for truth, for "authenticity", and for the total fulfilment of the individual human potential. But as this was something new in the history of mankind, the minds of the leaders of the movement could not adequately grasp it and soon started revolving again into their established grooves (like Marxism, structuralism, psychoanalysis, and often pure habitual verbalism). May '68 remains a one month's wonder which thinkers of all disciplines keep

---

89. The Mother: *Notes on the Way*, p. 1.
90. Luc Ferry and Alain Renaut: *La Pensée 68*, passim.

## 6. The Supramental "Catastrophe"

wondering about. Its authenticity is more and more confirmed by the fact that the sense of its importance grows ever stronger. It might be possible to comment on other historical facts from the second half of the 20th century and interpret them within the perspective sketched in these chapters, for instance the Watergate Affair and the oil crisis of 1973. We will limit ourselves, though, to that amazing year 1989 and the fall of the Berlin Wall together with the collapse of communism. One of the best eyewitness accounts of this extraordinary historical moment is Timothy Garton Ash's *We the People: The Revolution of '89 Witnessed in Warsaw, Budapest, Berlin and Prague*. We quote some passages from this well-informed, extremely interesting and heart-warming book.

"Should we talk about this [the 1989 events in Prague] as a revolution? someone asks. For after all, in our linguistic context the word 'revolution' has a clear subtext of violence. A 'peaceful revolution' sounds like a contradiction in terms. A rather academic point, you might think. But actually a great deal of what is happening is precisely about words: about finding new, plain, true words rather than the old mendacious phrases with which people have lived for so long." (p. 113) – "The motto of the year – and not just in Czechoslovakia – was *Pravda Vitezi*, the old Hussite slogan, adopted by Masaryk, 'Truth shall prevail', or, in the still more ancient Latin, *Magna est veritas et preavalebit* [the truth is great and will prevail]. As one talks in English of a 'moment of truth' for some undertaking, so this was a year of truth for communism. There is a real sense in which these regimes lived by the word and perished by the word." (p. 138) "Here, for the first time, we saw that massive, sustained, yet supremely peaceful and self-disciplined manifestation of social unity, the gentle crowd against the Party-state, which was both the hallmark and the essential domestic catalyst of change in 1989." (p. 133) – "I have found treasures: examples of great moral courage and intellectual integrity; comradeship, deep friendship, family life; time and space for serious conversation, music, literature, not disturbed by the perpetual noise of our media-driven and obsessively telecommunicative world;

Christian witness in its original and purest form; more broadly, qualities of relations between men and women of very different backgrounds, and once bitterly opposed faiths – an ethos of solidarity." (p. 154)

"The truth is that 1989 could have turned bloody at any point ... In Warsaw, we watched the first pictures from Tiananmen Square while waiting for the [decisive] election results. 'Tiananmen' was a word that I would hear muttered many times in Central and East European capitals over the next few months. What made the difference in Europe was two sets of political leaders: the opposition elites and the Gorbachev group in Moscow. 1989 was further proof of the vital importance of individuals in history." (p. 162)

And Timothy Garton Ash writes the following, for a critical-minded journalist, remarkable words which put the peaceful revolution of 1989 within the framework of the present chapter: "Yet when all this has been said, no one in Prague could resist the feeling that there must also be an additional, supra-rational cause at work. Hegel's *Weltgeist,* said some. [Saint] Agnes of Bohemia, said others. 'The whole world is moving from dictatorship to democracy', said a third ... How you describe the supra-rational agency is a matter of personal choice. For myself, I stick to the angels." (p. 128)

The collapse of communism in Europe and Russia, unforeseen and unforeseeable even a month before it happened, was entirely bloodless, except for some incidents in Rumania. Non-violence was, according to Garton Ash, "the first commandment of all Central European oppositions." It was "unlike all earlier revolutions." In 1957 the Mother had said: "Something has happened in the world's history which allows us to hope that a selection of humanity, a small number of beings, perhaps, is ready to be transformed into pure gold, and that they will be able to manifest *strength without violence, heroism without destruction, and courage without catastrophe* ... At the moment we are at a decisive turning-point in terrestrial history, once again. From every side I am asked: 'What is going to happen?' Everywhere there is anguish, expectation, fear. 'What is going to happen?

## 6. The Supramental "Catastrophe"

...' There is only one answer: 'If only man would consent to be spiritualised.'"[91]

The Supermind and the Consciousness of the Overman are established. They are acting to transform the world. So are Sri Aurobindo and the Mother, who will remain present throughout the third and fourth phases of their avataric Work: the period after their apparent departure and the period of the tangible accomplishment of their mission. The effects of these four divine Forces is incomprehensible, unfathomable for the human mind – as are the events these Forces are producing towards a realisation surpassing everything humans are able to imagine. All these are not the imaginings of the present writer: it is a summary of what the Mother said in the last years of her presence on the Earth, when the foundations of a new world had been laid and the results were, from then onwards, inevitable.

"The miracles that are happening are not what one might call 'literary' miracles, in the sense that they do not happen as in the stories. They are visible only to a very deep vision of things – very deep, very comprehensive, very broad. You must already be capable of following the methods and ways of the Grace in order to recognise its action. You must already be capable of not being blinded by appearances in order to see a deeper truth of things."[92]

---

91. The Mother: <u>Questions and Answers 1957-58</u>, pp. 73-74 (emphasis added).
92. Id., p. 246.

# 7

# The Future of Humanity

> *To hope for a true change of human life without a change of human nature is an irrational and unspiritual proposition; it is to ask for something unnatural and unreal, an impossible miracle.*[1]
>
> – SRI AUROBINDO

Some specimens of *homo sapiens* will, according to Sri Aurobindo and the Mother, evolve into transitional forms of overmen, who in their turn will render the appearance of the divine species of supramental beings and a new world order possible. "All life for the achieved spiritual or gnostic consciousness must be the manifestation of the realised truth of Spirit; only what can transform itself and find its own spiritual self in that greater Truth and fuse itself into its harmony can be accorded a life-acceptance", wrote Sri Aurobindo in *The Life Divine*. "What will survive the mind cannot determine, for the supramental gnosis will itself bring down its own truth and that truth will take up whatever of itself has been put forth in our ideals and realisations of mind and life and body. The forms it has taken there may not survive, for they are not likely to be suitable without change or replacement in the new existence; but what is real and abiding in them or even in their forms will undergo the transformation necessary for survival. Much that is normal to human life would disappear. In the light of gnosis the many mental idols, constructed principles and systems, conflicting ideals which man has created in all domains of his mind and life, could command no acceptance or reverence; only the

---

1. Sri Aurobindo: *The Life Divine*, p. 1059.

## 7. The Future of Humanity

truth, if any, which these specious images conceal, could have a chance of entry as elements of a harmony founded on a much wider basis."[2]

Sri Aurobindo, writing before the descent of the Supermind in 1956, had to write in the subjunctive tense. The Mother, speaking after '56 and having realised the overman, could use a much more affirmative mode and give us some certitude about the future developments, all of which will result from the present potentialities in humanity. It is therefore important to have a clear idea of humanity's constitution, which is much more complex than generally supposed. (The basic shortcoming in the socialist and Marxist systems, for instance, was that they totally misjudged human nature.)

All human beings may be equal before the law, but they are far from equal in their development and potential. "Inferior mankind gravitates downward from mind towards life and body; average mankind dwells constant in mind limited by and looking towards life and body; superior mankind levitates upward either to idealised mentality or to pure idea, direct truth of knowledge and spontaneous truth of existence; supreme mankind rises to divine beatitude and from that level either goes upwards to pure Sat and Parabrahman or remains to beatify its lower members and raise to divinity in itself and others this human existence."[3]

We have already drawn attention to the importance of the human mass, the massive body of humanity, which is the constant cause of man's "downward gravitation", and of the diminution and distortion of the ideas, values and standards discovered or acquired by individuals. "In the mass the collective consciousness is near to the inconscient; it has a subconscious, an obscure and mute movement which needs the individual to express it, to bring it to light, to organise it and make it effective. The mass-consciousness by itself moves by a vague, half-formed or unformed subliminal and commonly subconscient impulse rising to the surface; it is prone to a blind

---
2. Id., pp. 1065-66.
3. Sri Aurobindo: *Essays Divine and Human*, p. 102.

or half-seeing unanimity which suppresses the individual in the common movement: if it thinks, it is by the motto, the slogan, the watchword, the common crude or formed idea, the traditional, the accepted customary notion; it acts, when not by instinct or on impulse, then by the rule of the pack, the herd-mentality, the type-law."[4]

The same, according to Sri Aurobindo, goes for spirituality. "If [in the past] no decisive but only a contributory result, an accretion of some new finer elements to the sum of the consciousness, has been the general consequence and there has been no life-transformation, it is because man in the mass has always deflected the spiritual impulsion, recanted from the spiritual ideal or held it only as a form and rejected the inward change. Spirituality cannot be called upon to deal with life by a non-spiritual-method or attempt to cure its ills by the panaceas, the political, social or other mechanical remedies which the mind is constantly attempting and which have always failed and will continue to fail to solve anything. The most drastic changes made by these means change nothing; for the old ills exist in a new form: the aspect of the outward environment is altered, but man remains what he was; he is still an ignorant mental being misusing or not effectively using his knowledge, moved by ego and governed by vital desires and passions and the needs of the body, unspiritual and superficial in his outlook, ignorant of his own self and the forces that drive and use him."[5]

"It is pertinently suggested", writes Sri Aurobindo, "that if such an evolutionary culmination is intended and man is to be its medium, it will only be a few especially evolved human beings who will form the new type and move towards the new life; that once done, the rest of humanity will sink back from a spiritual aspiration no longer necessary for Nature's purpose and remain quiescent in its normal status. It can equally be reasoned that the human gradation must be preserved if there is really an ascent of the soul by reincarnation through the evolutionary

---

4. Sri Aurobindo: *The Life Divine*, p. 693.
5. Id., p. 884.

degrees towards the spiritual summit; for otherwise the most necessary of all the intermediate steps will be lacking. It must be conceded at once that there is not the least probability or possibility of the whole human race rising in a block to the supramental level. What is suggested is nothing so revolutionary and astonishing, but only the capacity in the human mentality, when it has reached a certain level or a certain point of stress of the evolutionary impetus, to press forward towards a higher plane of consciousness and its embodiment in the being."[6]

"Man is an abnormal who has not found his own normality, – he may imagine he has, he may appear to be normal in his own kind, but that normality is only a sort of provisional order; therefore, though man is infinitely greater than the plant or the animal, he is not perfect in his own nature like the plant and the animal. This imperfection is not a thing to be at all deplored, but rather a privilege and a promise, for it opens out to us an immense vista of self-development and self-exceeding. Man at his highest is a half-god who has risen out of the animal nature and is splendidly abnormal in it, but the thing which he has started out to be, the whole god, is something so much greater than what he is that it seems to him as abnormal to himself as he is to the animal. This means a great and arduous labour of growth before him, but also a splendid crown of his race and his victory. A kingdom is offered to him beside which his present triumphs in the realms of mind or over external Nature will appear as a rough hint and a poor beginning."[7]

Having considered this highly idealistic and simultaneously profoundly realistic view – which is the global Aurobindonian view – we are now ready to have a look at the kinds of higher species that, originating from and along with the human species, will people our transformed planet in the future.

---

6. Id., p. 842 (emphasis added.)
7. Sri Aurobindo: *The Human Cycle,* p. 234.

## The Future Mental and Supra-Mental Populations on Earth

As noted before, all future populations envisaged by Sri Aurobindo and the Mother will be developments of the present potential of humankind. One should always keep in mind Sri Aurobindo's warning that only the Supermind knows how things will evolve, and that future evolutions are unpredictable and even unimaginable to the contemporary human being. What follows is, however, based on the experience and foresight of Sri Aurobindo and the Mother themselves, and will be documented with quotations from their work.

*1. Animal-man.* The human condition as it has been ever since *homo sapiens* appeared is for an important part, not to say for the greatest part, determined by the fact that *homo sapiens* has inherited the animal characteristics of the primates, physically as well as in his sub-rational psychological make-up. This animal part of his constitution is dominated mainly by the lower vital and the subconscious. How badly rational man, the reasoning being, had overrated himself during the Age of Reason was appallingly proven by some of the main events of the 20th century. Until now, man has explored himself in only a very limited part of his real being, the most superficial part in fact, leaving unexplored the nether and the upper realms in which he also concretely exists.

Animal-man, "the most necessary of all the intermediate steps" as it is put in one of the quotations above, will continue existing as a species, which is not the same as saying that he will continue existing in the same numbers. His destiny is for the most part collective, although he is the first terrestrial being with a sense of individuality. "It is not indeed necessary or possible that the whole race should transform itself from mental into spiritual beings, but a general admission of the ideal, a widespread endeavour, a conscious concentration are needed to carry the stream of tendency to its definitive achievement. Otherwise what will be ultimately accomplished is an achievement by the few initiating a new order of beings, while humanity will

## 7. The Future of Humanity

have passed sentence of unfitness on itself and may fall back into an evolutionary decline or a stationary immobility; for it is the constant upward effort that has kept humanity alive and maintained for it its place in the front of creation."[8]

It is essential to keep in mind that, because of the presence of the supramental beings, the whole of the Earth, including the animals and animal-man, will change from a place of order into a place of contented existence. The Supermind is a Consciousness of Harmony, and this harmony, together with its spiritual basis, will be reflected in the whole of terrestrial existence. Freed from its inherent evolutionary impulse, the future animal-man will be satisfied within his limitations and share, as far as his capacities allow, in the universal wonders.

*2. Man-man.* This will be a species that has realised the full human potential, but without reaching for the spiritual levels above it. The Mother related her vision of this new species, a positive evolution from the animal-human species, as follows: "There was [in her experience of the future] the whole part of humanity that will no longer be altogether animal, that will have benefited from the mental development and created a certain harmony in its life – a vital and artistic, a cultural harmony – in which the large majority will be content to live. They have acquired a kind of harmony and within it they live life as it exists in a civilised environment, rather cultured, that is, with refined tastes and refined habits. And this whole way of life has a certain beauty in which they feel at ease; and unless something catastrophic happens to them, they are happy and contented, satisfied with life."

"Because these people have discernment, as they are intellectually developed, they may be attracted by the new forces, by that what is new, the future life. For example they may become disciples of Sri Aurobindo in a mental, intellectual way. But they do not feel at all the need to change physically, and if they were compelled to do so, it would in the first place be premature, unjust, and [secondly] it would simply cause a great disorder

---

8. Sri Aurobindo: *The Life Divine,* p. 724.

and disturb their life altogether uselessly."[9] It was typical of the Mother (as it was of Sri Aurobindo) that she never wanted to upset people's convictions. The "mental constructions" – her term – of a person, built up during this life on the basis of former lives, constitutes an integral part of his personality. Trying to change it without a profound understanding of its complexity and possibilities, is a delicate act and may dangerously unbalance a person for the rest of his ongoing existence. Fundamental change, the yoga of transformation, is only for the mature souls capable of undergoing the required tests and ordeals.

This vision of man-man "came after a vision of plants and their spontaneous beauty (it is something so wonderful), then of the animal with such a harmonious life so long as human beings do not come in between, and all that was in its right place. Then [there was the vision] of the true humanity as humanity, that is to say the maximum of what a mental equilibrium can create by way of beauty, harmony, charm, elegance of life and a taste for living – a taste for living in beauty – and of course excluding all that is ugly and low and vulgar. It was a beautiful humanity. Humanity at its maximum, but beautiful. And perfectly satisfied with being human, because it lives harmoniously. And this is perhaps also like a promise of what nearly the whole of humanity will become under the influence of the new creation. It looked to me that this was what the supramental consciousness could make of humanity ... It would be something that would have the power to eliminate all errors, all deformations, all the ugliness of the mental life, and [that] then [would be] a very happy humanity, totally satisfied with being human, not at all feeling the need of being anything else than human, but with a human beauty, a human harmony. It was very pleasant. It was as if I lived in it. The contradictions had disappeared. It was as if I lived in that perfection. And it was almost like the ideal conceived by the supramental Consciousness of a humanity become as perfect as it can be. And it was very good."[10]

---

9. The Mother: *Notes on the Way*, p. 24.
10. Id., pp. 25 ff.

## 7. The Future of Humanity

Sri Aurobindo too wrote about this "true humanity", even in his series of articles on overman: "The result of the supramental descent need not be limited to those who could thus open themselves entirely and it need not be limited to the supramental change; there could also be a minor or secondary transformation of the mental being within a freed and perfected scope of the mental nature. In place of the human mind as it now is, a mind limited, imperfect, open at every moment to all kinds of deviation from the truth or missing of the truth, all kinds of error and openness even to the persuasions of a complete falsehood and perversion of the nature ... there could emerge a true mind liberated and capable of the free and utmost perfection of itself and its instruments, a life governed by the free and illumined mind, a body responsive to the light and able to carry out all that the free mind and will could demand of it.

"This change might happen not only in the few, but extend and generalise itself in the race. This possibility, if fulfilled, would mean that the human dream of perfection, perfection of itself, of its purified and enlightened nature, of all its ways of action and living, would be no longer a dream but a truth that could be made real and humanity lifted out of the hold on it of inconscience and ignorance. The life of the mental being could be harmonised with the life of the Supermind which will then be the highest order above it, and become even an extension and annexe of the Truth-consciousness, a part and province of the divine life ... An immense change of human life, even if it did not extend to transformation, would be inevitable."[11]

"In the untransformed part of humanity itself there might well arise a new and greater order of mental human beings; for the directly intuitive or partly intuitivised but not yet gnostic [i.e. supramentalised] mental being, the directly or partly illumined mental being, the mental being in direct or part communion with the higher-thought plane would emerge; these would become more and more numerous, more and more evolved and secure in their type, and might even exist as a formed race

---

11. Sri Aurobindo: *Essays Divine and Human*, pp. 565-66.

of higher humanity leading upwards the less evolved in a true fraternity born of the sense of the manifestation of the One Divine in all beings."[12]

"This opens up roads of realisation into the future", said the Mother, "possibilities that are already foreseen, when an entire part of humanity, the one which is open consciously or unconsciously to the new forces, will be elevated, as it were, into a higher, more harmonious, more perfect life. Even if in that case individual transformation is not always permissible or possible, there will be a kind of general uplifting, a harmonisation of the whole, which will make it possible that a new order, a new harmony will be established, and that the anguish of the present disorder and struggles will disappear and be replaced by an order allowing a harmonious functioning of the whole.

"There will be other consequences which will tend to eliminate in an opposite way what the intervention of the mind in life has created: perversion, ugliness, a whole mass of distortions that have increased the suffering, the misery, the moral poverty – an entire area of sordid and repulsive misery which turns a great part of human life into something so horrible. This is what must disappear. This is what makes humanity in so many ways infinitely inferior to the animal life in its simplicity and in the natural spontaneity and harmony that it has in spite of everything. Suffering in animals is never so miserable and sordid as it is in an entire section of humanity that has been perverted by the use of a mentality utilised exclusively for egoistic needs." The Mother concludes: "We must rise beyond, emerge into the Light and the Harmony, or fall back below, into the simplicity of a healthy animal life without perversions."[13]

3. *Overman*. Overman, according to the Mother's definition, is a being born from animal-human parents, as have been all humans in past ages and as they still are today, but who will develop a partly supramentalised consciousness, a Mind of Light. This kind of being will make possible the transition from

---
12. Sri Aurobindo: *The Life Divine*, p. 1012.
13. The Mother: <u>Questions and Answers 1957-58</u>, pp. 298-99.

## 7. The Future of Humanity

the human to the supramental species. As the Mother said in April 1972: "The change from the human into the supramental being is being achieved ... through the overman. It may be that there will be some overmen – *there are some* – who will make the transition possible."[14]

Another quotation from the Mother worth repeating in order to imprint it into the memory of all those "who look in the same direction" of a new World, is the following from 1958, when she had accomplished the realisation of the overman: "All those who make an effort to overcome their ordinary nature, all those who try to realise materially the profound experience that has brought them into contact with the divine Truth, all those who, instead of turning to the Hereafter or the On-high, try to realise physically, externally, the change of consciousness they have realised within themselves – all those are apprentice-overmen. Among them, there are countless variations in the success of their efforts. Each time we try not to be an ordinary man, not to live the ordinary life, to express in our movements, our actions and reactions the divine Truth, when we are governed by that Truth instead of being governed by the general ignorance, we are apprentice-overmen, and according to the success of our efforts we are, well, more or less good apprentices, more or less advanced on the way."

Where are they, then, these apprentice-overmen and apprentice-overwomen? For those related to the Work of Sri Aurobindo and the Mother, the first place to look for them is in themselves. Overman or overwoman may be in embryo there. As wrote Nolini Kanta Gupta, one of the close collaborators of Sri Aurobindo and the Mother: "Although we may not know it, the New Man – the divine race of humanity – is already among us. It may be in our next neighbour, in our nearest brother, even in myself. Only a thin veil covers it. It marches just behind the line. It waits for an occasion to throw off the veil and place itself in the forefront."[15] These are important words from a yogi in

---
14. See, once again, Georges Van Vrekhem: *Overman: The Intermediary between the Human and the Supramental Being* (Rupa & Co).
15. Printed above his signature in *Sri Aurobindo Mandir Annual* 1987.

one of whose birthday cards the Mother wrote: *En route vers le surhomme* – on the way towards the overman.[16] The occasion to throw off the veil may be one of the unexpected events the future has in store, for "this is the time of the unexpected." "Now we will see", said the Mother.

4. *The supramental being.* To start and lay the foundations of the supramental transformation of the Earth was the mission of Sri Aurobindo and the Mother. The expectation of a new species beyond man is entirely logical if one accepts the following premises: a) that all is the Brahman, and b) that the Earth, like the universe it spins through, is a field of evolution. The surprising fact may be that the new, higher species, beyond man should appear *now*. For it is typical of man's curious psychological set-up, conservative out of egoism, ignorance, and fear, that all important evolutionary events are supposed to have taken place in the past, and that the heralds of a new development on that planet always have been violently countered in the name of the past.

That something is taking place *now* is undeniable by anyone able to take a step back from the events in recent history and to examine them with an unprejudiced eye. *This* has never happened before: the growing unification of humanity; a staggering increase of the global population; the establishing of means of worldwide communication, which in its complexity begins to resemble a kind of global nervous system; the emergence of a global awareness; an ever expanding penetration and knowledge of new fields of knowledge, of our macrocosmic environment and the subatomic constitution of Matter, a tendency towards equality of the sexes and of all human beings; an empathy for the animals, our companion species on the planet, and for Mother Earth herself ... All this is coming about in an incredibly short time, indicating that it is no longer a matter of evolution but of evolutionary revolution, of evolutionary explosion.

"There is nothing in this future evolution of the being which could be regarded as irrational or incredible", wrote Sri

---

16. In *Homage to Nolini Kanta Gupta*, p. 21.

Aurobindo in *The Life Divine*, "there is nothing in it abnormal or miraculous: it would be the necessary course of the evolution of consciousness and its forces in the passage from the mental to the gnostic or supramental formulation of our existence. This action of the forces of Supernature would be a natural, normal and spontaneously simple working of the new higher or greater consciousness into which the being enters in the course of his self-evolution; the gnostic being accepting the gnostic life would develop and use the powers of this greater consciousness, even as man develops and uses the powers of his mental nature."[17]

## Cleaning up the Mess

> *The Supramental is independent of conditions and circumstances.*[18]
>
> – Sri Aurobindo

The condition of our overpopulated Earth at present is far from reassuring; actually, many hold that the point of no return has been reached and that spaceship Earth is sailing towards its doom. Then does it still make sense to look forward to the coming of a new species? Will this be materially possible?

In the view of Sri Aurobindo and the Mother, it is precisely the presence of the Supramental Force that will save the planet, just as all great disturbances, recent and contemporary, have been caused by its preparation and descent. In the first place: "The Earth will not perish", asserted the Mother forcefully.[19] In the second place: "In Nature there are no errors", wrote Sri Aurobindo, "but only the deliberate measure of her paces traced and retraced in a prefigured rhythm, of which each step has a meaning and its place in the action and reaction of her spiritual

---

17. Sri Aurobindo: *The Life Divine*, pp. 1042-43.
18. Nirodbaran: *Talks with Sri Aurobindo* II, p. 314.
19. The Mother: *Notes on the Way*, p. 7.

advance." To Sri Aurobindo "Nature" was always the great Executrix of the divine Will in its manifestation, and as such the divine Will itself. "We may be sure that if destruction is done, it is because for that end the destruction was indispensable."[20]

As the Supermind is a principle of harmony and beauty, the continued existence of a mess like the one created by man-the-mental-being is impossible. "The presence of the liberated and now sovereign supramental light and force at the head of evolutionary Nature might be expected to have its consequences in the whole evolution, an incidence, a decisive stress would affect the life of the lower evolutionary stages; something of the light, something of the force would penetrate downwards and awaken into a greater action the hidden Truth-Power everywhere in Nature. A dominant principle of harmony would impose itself on the life of the Ignorance."[21] "A gnostic being will possess not only a truth-conscious control of the realised Spirit's power over its physical world, but also the full power of the mental and vital planes and the use of their greater forces for the perfection of the physical existence. This greater knowledge and wider hold of all existence will enormously increase the power of instrumentation of the gnostic being on his surroundings and on the world of physical Nature."[22]

"At the same time the involved principle of the gnosis, acting now as an overt, arisen and constantly dynamic force and no longer only as a concealed power with a secret origination or a veiled support of things or an occasional intervention as its only function, would be able to lay something of its law of harmony on the still existing Inconscience and Ignorance. For the secret gnostic power concealed in them would act with a greater strength of its support and origination, a freer and more powerful intervention; the beings of the Ignorance, influenced by the light of the gnosis through their association with gnostic beings and through the evolved and effective presence of the

---

20. Sri Aurobindo: *The Human Cycle*, p. 369.
21. Sri Aurobindo: *The Life Divine*, p. 96.
22. Id., p. 980.

## 7. The Future of Humanity

supramental Being and Power in earth-nature, would be more conscious and responsive."[23]

It is not for nothing that the historians scratch their heads in vain to find some meaning in or behind the present developments in the world: to them and to most others all significant facts are negative, or uninterpretable, or unprecedented, or absurd. And life is so full and so fast that many may feel that there is no time left to find out what Sri Aurobindo and the Mother actually have said and who they factually have been. But *if* one takes the time to find this out, then it is difficult to deny that their view, their conclusions and their predictions concur on all points with the facts of the last century and of the present situation. Prolonging these lines, then, may very well lead towards the New World they stood and stand for. The present darkness would then only be apparent, for, according to them, the Light behind and within is already there.

"This is the problem that is put to us now: with the addition, with the new help of the [supramental] Force that has descended, that is manifesting, that is working, why shouldn't one take up this enormous game [of Nature] to make it more beautiful, more harmonious, more true? It only needs brains powerful enough to receive the Force and formulate the possible course of action. There must be consciousnesses powerful enough to convince Nature that there are other methods than hers."

"This looks like madness, but all new things have always seemed madness before they became realities. The hour has come for *this* madness to be realised. And since we are all here for reasons perhaps unknown to most of you, but nonetheless very conscious reasons, we may set ourselves to accomplish this madness. At least it will be worthwhile living it."[24] Thus spoke the Mother.

---

23. Id., p. 1012.
24. The Mother: *Questions and Answers 1957-58*, pp. 35-36.

## Note About the Sources

The first edition of Sri Aurobindo's writings was published thirty years ago, in view of his birth centenary in 1972, and appropriately called "Sri Aurobindo Birth Centenary Library" (SABCL).

At the time of writing this book, a new revised and augmented edition of Sri Aurobindo's writings is being published: "The Complete Works of Sri Aurobindo" (CWSA), but many volumes of this new edition are still awaiting publication.

This puts the writer in the uncomfortable position of having to quote from two sets of Sri Aurobindo's works. The reader interested in retracing the sources should therefore know to which set of works the quoted writings belong.

To the "Sri Aurobindo Birth Centenary Library" belong:

> *Collected Poems* (vol. 5)
> *The Upanishads* (vol. 12)
> *The Life Divine* (vol. 18 and 19)
> *Letters on Yoga* (vol. 22, 23 and 24)
> *On the Mother* (vol. 25)
> *On Himself* (vol. 26)

To "The Complete Works of Sri Aurobindo" belong:

> *Essays Divine and Human* (vol. 12)
> *Essays in Philosophy and Yoga* (vol. 13)
> *Essays on the Gita* (vol. 19)
> *The Synthesis of Yoga* (vol. 23 and 24)
> *The Human Cycle* (vol. 25)
> *Savitri* (vol. 33 and 34).

All quoted works of the Mother belong to the centenary edition of the "Collected Works of the Mother" (CWM), and have been checked against the original French edition.

*Biographical Note*

Georges Van Vrekhem (°1935) is a Flemish speaking Belgian who writes in English. He became known in his country as a journalist, poet and playwright. For some time he was the artistic manager of a professional theatre company. He gave numerous talks and presentations in America, Europe and India. He became first acquainted with the works of Sri Aurobindo and the Mother in 1964. In 1970 he joined the Sri Aurobindo Ashram in Pondicherry, and in 1978 he became a member of Auroville, where he is still living and writing.

He wrote:

*Beyond Man, the Life and Work of Sri Aurobindo and The Mother* (1997)

*The Mother, the Story of Her Life* (2000)

*Overman, the Intermediary between the Human and the Supramental Being* (2000)

*Patterns of the Present, in the Light of Sri Aurobindo and the Mother* (2001)

*The Mother: the Divine Shakti* (2003)

*Hitler and His God – The Background to the Nazi Phenomenon* (2006)

*Evolution, Religion, and the Unknown God* (2011)

Books by him are translated into Dutch, French, German, Italian, Russian, and Spanish. He was awarded the Sri Aurobindo Puraskar for 2006 by the Government of Bengal.

Printed in Great Britain
by Amazon